D0518697

SCOTLAND IN FOCUS

Scotland in Focus

Photography by Keith Allardyce

Text by Kristina Woolnough

HarperCollins*Publishers*

HarperCollins Publishers
PO Box, Glasgow G4 0NB

First Published 1992

ISBN 0 00 435651 9

Reprint 9 8 7 6 5 4 3 2 1 0

A catalogue record for this book is available from the British Library.

Printed in Hong Kong

Contents

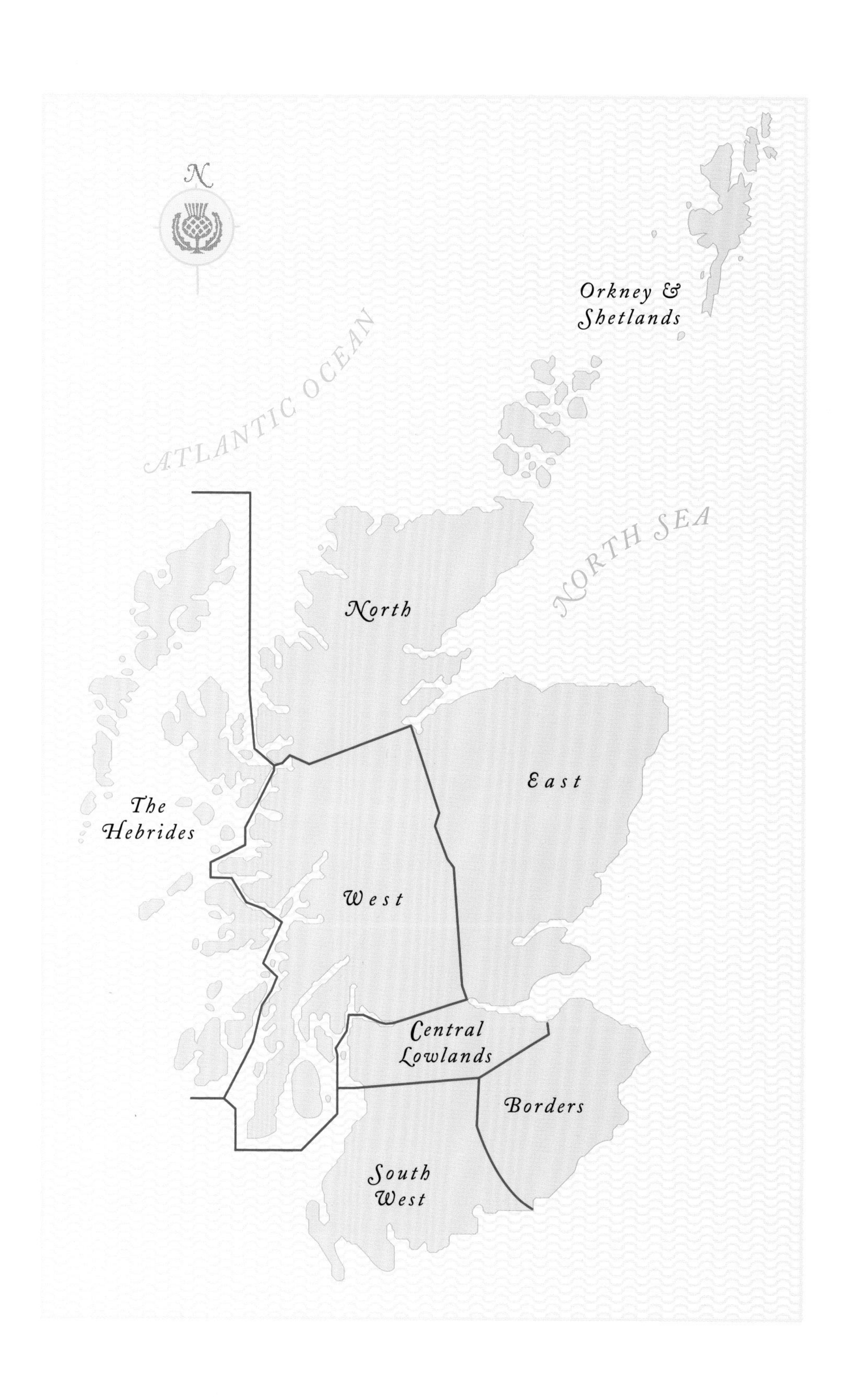
N
Orkney &
Shetlands
ATLANTIC OCEAN
NORTH SEA
North
East
The
Hebrides
West
Central
Lowlands
Borders
South
West

Introduction

Scotland, perhaps more than any other country in the world, is a country enmeshed in its past. Its landscape is littered with reminders, places where battles were won and lost, the ruins of sacked or abandoned castles, towns and villages which have been settlements since the Iron Age. Scotland's culture has fed voraciously on its history too: there is an abundance of folk songs, literature, theatre and art which hark back to pre-Union times of independence and pride. Indeed, it is perhaps this determined nostalgia that has ensured Scotland's individuality and distinctiveness in the face of such 20th century uniformities as leisure complexes, chain stores and the global rash of fast-food outlets. Scotland has these too, but they are hardly a dot on the map in comparison with the country's vast historical and geographical wealth.

That richness is what makes Scotland so remarkably photogenic. Whether mountains flaunt their snowy caps against bright blue skies, or whether the climate is sulky and drizzly, Scotland is always easy to identify in photographs. A jamboree of tartan, bagpipes and Highland games is accompanied by the coolly reflective waters of lochs and the smouldering grandeur of mountains draped in mist. There are less familiar images of less familiar places too, and some of these images reveal the new emergent Scotland. Glasgow, now bursting with pride in its Victorian finery, is the diamond in that crown. Towns and villages across the country are following Glasgow's lead. From East Lothian mining settlements to the fishing villages of the north east, there has been a decline in demand for traditional industries. Those places, like Glasgow, have had to struggle to find a replacement, both for their respective economies and for their local pride. Modern Scotland is challenging and exciting. Festivals abound, contemporary arts and crafts are flourishing and tourism, too often the black sheep industry, is being looked at with fresh eyes.

The things that have brought visitors to Scotland again and again – the dramatic, ever-changing landscape, the romantic appeal of its myths and legends, and the craggy splendour of its castles – are now more accessible and are now complemented by new attractions. Heritage trails crisscross the land, signposting Scotland's best for visitors, and purpose-built centres explain everything from whisky and the Loch Ness monster to Culloden. Although not always architecturally appealing, these centres do at least fully involve the visitor in Scotland's story.

That story is characterised by an independence of spirit and a fierce individuality. It is, however, important to slide away from Scotland generalisations, if only to realise that the country unravels like Chinese boxes. For under the umbrella nationhood of Scotland, each area, town and village is, and feels itself to be, quite distinctive too. And as you explore Scotland, whether as a native or as a visitor, you will realise that the more you discover, the more there is to know.

Kristina Woolnough 1992

Border countryside

The Borders

The dark inky cartographer's line that separates England and Scotland is, not without justification, a nervously shaky one. As if aware that the land above and below Scotland's irregular hemline was for centuries the subject of a bloody Scotland-versus-England tug-of-war, it wobbles uncertainly from Gretna in the west through Carter Bar and Coldstream. It then follows the River Tweed nearly all the way to the east coast. But before it smells the salty air of the North Sea, the borderline takes a sudden lurch northwards, turning away from the Tweed and the seaside resort of Berwick-upon-Tweed.

Berwick-upon-Tweed was, and continues to be, a focal point for the territorial struggle. Although arguably a geographical illogicality, the town now lies in the political realm of Northumberland, England, despite the occasional nationalist voices that call for its return to Scottish dominion.

Fortunately for the tourist board that promotes them, the Scottish Borders proper, frontierland and gateway, are sprinkled with the magnetic physical and cultural evidence of this past conflict. Surly defensive castles, stern fortified houses and innocently grassy battlefields now prove prime visitor attractions. The strife has provided another legacy—the summer festivals, or common ridings, of Borders towns which, with their processions, horse racing, pageants and ridings of the marches, invariably involve some territorial demarcation. Traditional ballads and Sir Walter Scott's novels, full of romantic heroics and dastardly deeds, add to the compulsive fire and pathos of the area.

Coldstream and Gretna Green, two of the inhabited Scotland-England thresholds, are charged with romance of another kind. Both gave refuge and marriage licences to eloping lovers who were too young to marry in England. The Old Blacksmith's Shop in Gretna Green is still a mecca for coachloads of those beguiled by the desperate promise of love on the run. Grateful letters from underage lovers joined in wedlock (for a fee) over the blacksmith's anvil deck the walls. Reading these tales of Romance Victorious, modern-day couples squeeze each other's hands and bill and coo. They then emerge into the shop proper to be seduced by lucky horseshoes (in small or medium sizes), and miniature lucky anvils. There, the only ring of any consequence is the ring of the till.

The traffic-gorged A74, a short distance from Gretna Green, is the west coast route into Scotland. It travels to Glasgow, through the political region of Dumfries and Galloway. This region, although primarily containing south west Scotland, also nibbles into Borders country. In the stolen Dumfries and Galloway sliver to the east of the A74, Moffat, which lies at the edge of the Tweedsmuir Hills and below the cavernous hollow of the Devil's Beef Tub, undoubtedly has the sedate, long-established aspect of a Borders town.

Outside Carlisle, the A7 strikes off diagonally into Scotland, heading at an angle for Edinburgh and the east. In the process, it strings together three of the best-known Borders towns—Galashiels, Selkirk and Hawick.

Galashiels, the most northerly of the three, lies in a crease in the high, rounded hummocks of the Southern Uplands, only 34 miles from Edinburgh. The rolling green hills around Galashiels are voluptuous. Mostly bald, but with occasional toupees, sideburns and tufts of trees, they sweep up from the River Gala in ample, generous curves. By contrast Galashiels seems stern. Its older buildings are dressed in uncompromising grey stone, its younger ones in the less dignified brick and corrugated iron clothing of the 20th century. The town's manufacturing traditions and its mighty reputation as a hub of trading in wool and textiles have exacted a price on its visual appearance. Galashiels is not pretty in the conventional sense; yet its run-down mills and dilapidated warehouses nonetheless serve as a workhorse monument to the town's achievements.

Selkirk wears its wool and tweed mantle somewhat more attractively. A hillside of houses, with mill chimneys poking up from the valley floor, Selkirk town centre is compact and appealing. Easily walkable, the main street represents something that the seems typically Borders—a comfortable blend of the traditions of rural living with contemporary accessories. The town's small, triangular market place boasts the Selkirk Bannock Shop and a statue of Sir Walter Scott, given a bizarre coat of pale grey gloss paint. Sir Walter is counterbalanced at the end of the High Street by another statue, of explorer Mungo Park, also dressed top-to-toe in dove grey. Historically and touristically, Selkirk is closely associated with disastrous Battle of Flodden of 1513 after which a captured English banner was paraded around the town, an event which is recalled each year in Selkirk's Common Riding.

Over more undulating hills striped with 'stone hedges' as Dr Johnson called the dry-stane dykes, and you enter Hawick, the self-dubbed 'home of knitwear'. The handsome, honey-coloured sandstone houses of Hawick, the largest Border town, fill a well between hills. Built for power, like most of the wool-industry towns, on one or other of the many tributaries of the Tweed, Hawick is spliced by the Teviot. As in other Border textile towns, the riverside location has a scenic potential which is only now being realised. For the most part, the Teviot winds through the town, largely uncelebrated, diving under dilapidated mill warehouses advertising seemingly never-ending clearance sales. Change, however, is in the air as abandoned warehouses are being adapted with enthusiasm and are being revitalised as the homes of craft workshops.

With Selkirk and Hawick, Jedburgh and Melrose form an easily-negotiable quadrilateral of Borders towns. The latter two are joined by the A68, which crosses into Scotland high up in the Cheviot Hills at Carter Bar, the most spectacular of the Scottish front doorsteps. Both Jedburgh and Melrose play host to the dramatic ruins of 12th-century abbeys. These abbeys, like the one at Dryburgh where Scott is buried, are made of sandstone which flushes through the red colour spectrum, from salmon pink to salami brown.

Melrose is genteel, a pleasing town of dried flowers and brasseries. Its tourist attractions are easily accessible. Melrose Abbey, where the heart of Robert the Bruce reputedly lies, and Priorwood Gardens are within a fisherman's cast of one another. Here too is the inevitable crafts shop, stocked like hundreds of others across Scotland with china sheepdogs and mass-produced tartan rugs.

Close to Melrose, on the right bank of the Tweed, is Abbotsford House, a model of the exuberance of

19th-century Romanticism. All turrets and crow-stepped gables, this was the home that Sir Walter Scott designed for himself, at great expense, and which is still owned by his descendants. During the summer months, Scottophiles come in pilgrimage to visit the library where Scott wrote *Rob Roy*, *The Heart of Midlothian* and *Old Mortality*. They see too his odd collection of memorabilia, including Robert Burns' drinking cup and Rob Roy's purse.

Another place of homage is Scott's View, further east along the Tweed valley. You chase a twisty road to a smooth summit, and the view is tremendous. The panorama, detailed on an etched plate fixed to a weathered stone plinth, stretches across fields with soil the shade of dried blood to Melrose and its lumpy bodyguards, the Eildon Hills. Down below the steady Tweed curves confidently around geographical obstacles, its banks maintaining a perfect parallel.

Despite the river's apparent opulence, several of the blue threads of the region's river system, inspirational for fishermen and poets, have yet to join it. Unspooling from the ranges of hills which cup the Borders towns, trickling and rushing through crevices and cracks in the flanks of the Southern Uplands and the Cheviot Hills, the Teviot, the Yarrow, the Gala Water and the Ettrick Water of the poet James Hogg will all eventually be subsumed by the Tweed.

At the junction of the Teviot and the Tweed lies Kelso. Sir Walter Scott, whose descriptions, pronouncements, fictional characters and novelistic locations dot the whole of the Borders region like dandelions, rhapsodized about Kelso, claiming it was 'the most beautiful, if not the most romantic village in Scotland'. Its abbey, the cobbled streets around its large, un-Scottish town square and the Georgian elegance of its buildings are indeed admirable, even if the tasteless canteen-beige plant tubs which litter the square somewhat ruin the effect.

The near-forest of signs directing the way to Kelso's rugby ground point to one of the Borders' sporty obsessions. Another, highlighted by Kelso's racecourse, is 'horsieculture'; gymkhanas, galas, point-to-point and fox-hunting thrive in the Borders. The costly round of lavish society hunt balls throws up an uncomfortable contrast with the more modest offerings of the dour-looking, ominously windowless dancing hall of Galashiels.

On the outskirts of Kelso is Floors Castle, a vast, imposing baronial pile fronted by equally imposing wrought-iron gates. Built to a William Adam design in 1721, it joins in the motto-making game of superlatives with gusto, claiming to be the largest inhabited house in Scotland. At the upper reaches of the Tweed near Innerleithen, Traquair House meanwhile publicizes itself as the oldest inhabited house in Scotland.

As the Tweed pushes on to the sea, so the landscape increasingly opens up and lies down. From Dryburgh eastwards, agricultural flatlands predominate. Roads are edged with beech and hawthorn and pheasants scuttle in front of cars while on the Berwickshire coast, yet another world exists.

Off the A1, the most easterly route into Scotland, Eyemouth makes its bread and butter as a commercial fishing village and as a seaside resort. A point on the Fishing Heritage Trail, its ungainly trawlers line up in the harbour beside the seaweed-smeared harbour road. With an oceanic pun which would have been worthy of Moby Dick, an Eyemouth hotel called The Contented Soul shows a flare of fishy humour. Beside the rocky natural harbour is a small arc of pale-mandarin sand, frequented by tiny buckets and spades in summer.

From Eyemouth, a coastal walk takes you to St Abbs, where the deep red of the sandstone buildings is highlighted by mortar picked out in white. The nature reserve and seacliffs of St Abb's Head act as harbingers for the solitude and middle-weight drama of the East Lothian coast of rocky bays and large crescents of white sand that comes next.

Even from the A1, the views of the North Sea, whether in milky blue or dangerous grey mood, are spectacular. At right-angles to the busy, lorry-congested trunk route are narrow roads which will draw you into the flat, fertile farmland and the picturesque villages and towns of East Lothian. Often commuter zones for Edinburgh or seaside playgrounds for Edinburghers, the most endearing feature of East Lothian is the warm blush of red sandstone and pink-stained soil. Lying beside the North Sea, Dunbar and North Berwick are both extraordinarily pink, as if coloured by a never-ending sunset. Tantallon Castle, dramatically perched right on the edge of seacliffs between the two royal burghs, is equally rosy.

In the midst of East Lothian's overwhelmingly flat terrain, North Berwick is in proud possession of two of the area's few protuberances and landmarks. The Bass Rock, a volcanic plug made piebald by guano, rises out of the sea to the right of North Berwick while behind the town lies North Berwick Law, topped by a whale jawbone arch and the crumbs of a ruin.

Haddington, Tyninghame, East Linton, Aberlady, Gullane and Dirleton complete the complement of admired East Lothian settlements. This is primarily red sandstone and Dutch orange pantile country, where villages are cosily and sometimes smugly picturesque and where civic-minded persons have launched Neighbourhood Watch schemes with gusto.

There are enough specific attractions—including Hailes Castle, the 17th-century Preston Mill with its roof like a bent-over wizard's hat, and the Phantassie Doocot (all near East Linton)—to encourage a swarm of weekend-jaunt visitors to flee the capital, and to wrestle with the frustrations of A1 traffic, in search of the rural idyll.

Detail from Samye Ling Tibetan Centre, Eskdalemuir (above)
A view from Carter Bar (opposite, top)
Riding the marches, Coldstream (opposite, bottom)

CALVERT
BRISTOL
TIPPED CIGARETTES

NO SMOKING

Manderston House, near Duns (opposite, top)
The stables, Manderston House (opposite, bottom)
The dairy, Manderston House (above)

Weaver, Hawick (top)
Glass-blower, Selkirk (bottom)
St Mary's Loch, Ettrick Forest (opposite)

Floors Castle, with detail from the main entrance gates (opposite)
Traquair House (above)

Scott's View, Bemersyde Hill (top)
Sir Walter Scott's death mask, Abbotsford House (bottom left)
The library, Abbotsford House (bottom right)

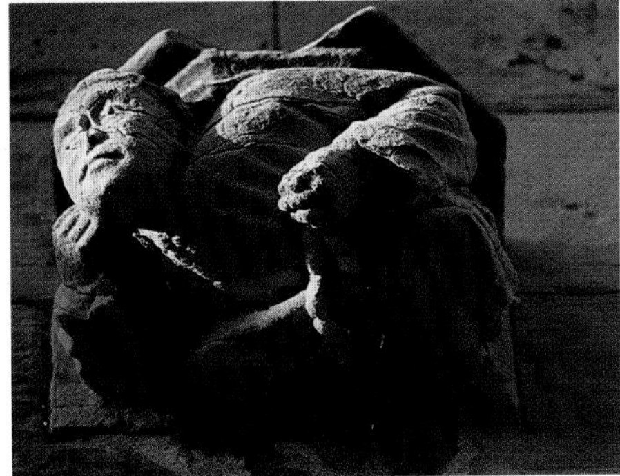

Dryburgh Abbey (top)
Melrose Abbey details (right)

HOTEL
DEVOTION
HARTLEPOOL

St Mary's Church and the River Tyne, Haddington (opposite, top)
Eyemouth harbour (opposite, bottom)
St Abbs (above)

St Abbs harbour (above)
Gannet colony, Bass Rock (opposite)

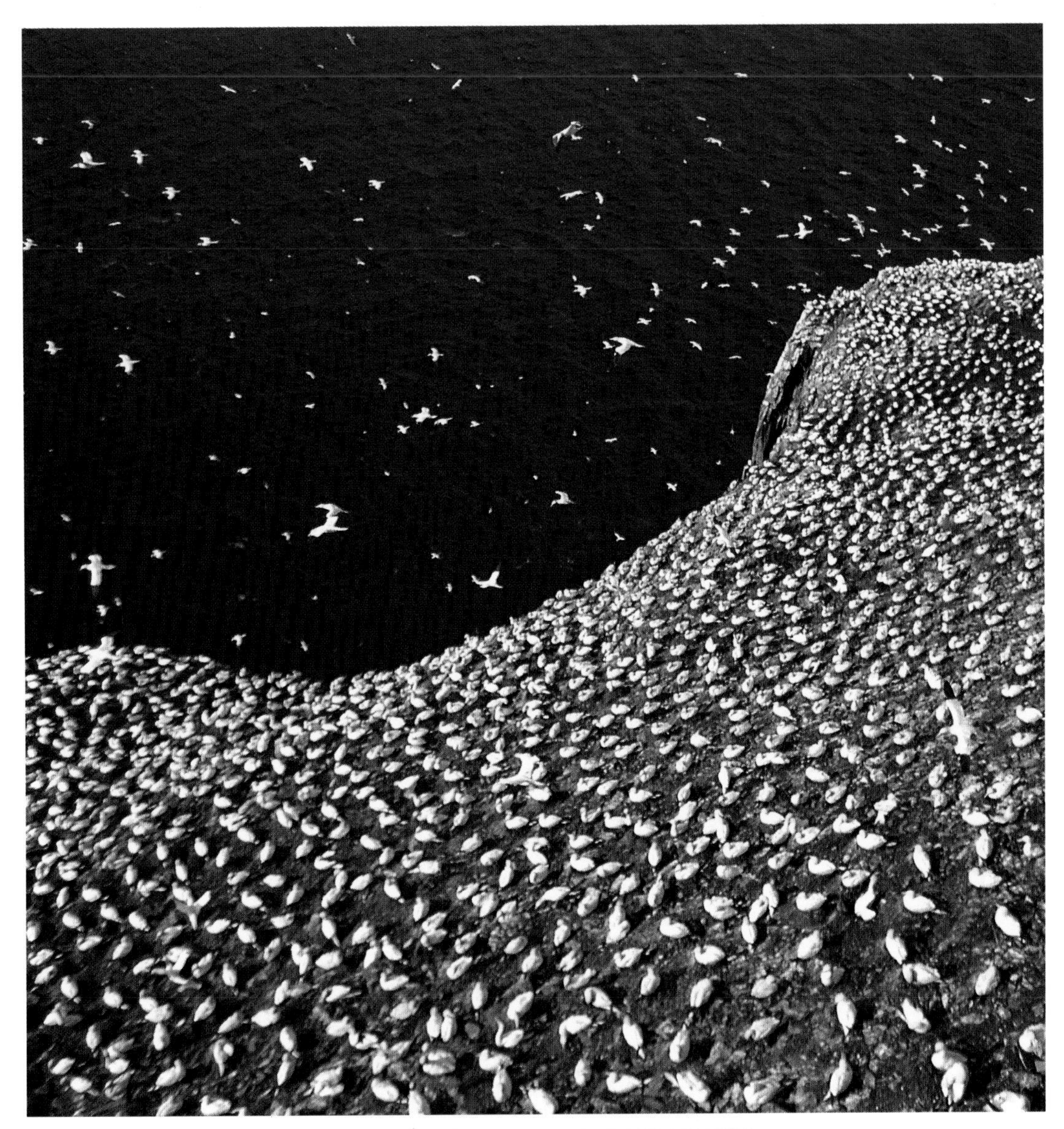

Gravestone, Sweetheart Abbey, New Abbey

The South West

'Oh, the flummery of a birthplace! Cant! Cant! Cant! It is enough to give a spirit the guts-ache.' Only 22 years after the death of Robert Burns, the Alloway cottage where he was born had already become a place to pay homage and possibly an entrance fee. Keats, visiting in 1818 and crying 'cant', was appalled. Unaware that he too would be the object of such flummery (his Hampstead home is now an attraction for London visitors), Keats was indignant about the whole concept, indignant despite the fact that he was, like many before and after him, pursuing the Burns trail that crawls over the face of south-west Scotland.

In 1803, the Wordsworths had put Burns' residences on the itinerary of *de rigueur* Romantic journeys. They came to Ayrshire and Dumfriesshire in search of the natural scenes that they believed had inspired Scotland's national poet. The Wordsworths mistakenly struggled to squeeze Burns into their invidious image of the ultimate 'noble savage': the poor-boy-made-good, the callus-handed labourer blessed with and uplifted by the feathery wings of poesy.

Instead of treading the delightful path of poetic fancy that she had expected, Dorothy Wordsworth was not, on the whole, impressed. The second Burns home in Dumfries, which was at that time still inhabited by Mrs Burns, prompted a weary sight of distaste: 'It has a mean appearance and is dirty about the doors as most Scotch houses are.' She droops with pity for Burns: 'We could think of little else but poor Burns, and his moving about that unpoetic ground.'

The cult of Burns worship that worried Keats was also of concern to the Orcadian poet Edwin Muir. In his 1935 travelogue *Scottish Journey*, he complains bitterly of the terrible queues at the Alloway cottage. He is unhappy that Burns' supposedly rural childhood snug is now parked beside the main road – 'in a suburban street, it was one of the most ludicrous and pathetic sights in Scotland.' But, whatever the assault on the sensibilities of the objectors or their sniffiness, visitors still flood to the squat, thatched, whitewashed but-and-ben.

Stooping to get through the door, these pilgrims tramp across the flag-stone floors to peer into the cubby-hole bed where the poet was born. They wonder at the rather unlikely 18th-century turnip-sowing machine, the cheese press and the pair of curling stones 'found in Ayr'. And they line up to sign the visitors' book before entering the small Burns museum, home to Burns' pistols and his waistcoat buttons.

The Burns Heritage Trail, undoubtedly a major attraction in this relatively unexplored pocket of

Scotland, loops from Ayr down to Dumfries and back up to Kilmarnock. Tourists are egged on from one Burnsiana outpost to the next, bringing their teatowel and postcard pennies to several villages, towns and Burns' centres. Such are the advantages of having a roving national poet.

Ayr, busy royal burgh and the largest of the Clyde seaside resorts, sports one of a number of Burns statues in Burns country (which includes a slice of Strathclyde Region and much of Dumfries and Galloway). Striking a Napoleonic stance on his pedestal, the poet admires the Volvos and Fords inside the Burns Statue Garage showroom down below. Lost amid the 20th-century hustle and bustle of Ayr's shoulder-to-shoulder chain stores is the Tam O'Shanter Museum which celebrates the eponymous hero of Burns' epic poem.

Ayr's Burnsian relics, its picturesque Auld Kirk and Auld Brig, and the flotillas of graceful swans which sail along the river are its traditional attractions. These are now joined by horse racing and by Wonderwest World, Scotland's answer to Disneyland. The town's seafront is endearingly British, a zone of weary pleasure inhabited by a Station for Lost Children, a decrepit pavilion half-heartedly advertising 'rock discos and big band sounds', and icecream vans emitting plaintive jingles. The seafront's charm is a wistful, hopeful one, one that is going to be defeated, if not by the British weather, then by the glossy allure of the Mediterranean.

Ayr's seaside resort near-neighbours, Prestwick and Troon, are different in character. Troon, famous for its verdant golf links, wears a silk headscarf of superiority. Well-kept, elegant and self-assured, it contrasts interestingly with Prestwick. Formerly Scotland's only landing-pad for airborne transatlantic visitors, Prestwick, like Girvan further down the west coast, wears the fixed grin of a town where pleasure is laid on but is not always successful. Hotels, guesthouses and nursing homes proliferate, as do betting shops, fish-and-chip bars and video rental outlets. Ayr, less a slave to incomers' pleasure and more a regional shopping centre, fits in somewhere between the two.

Just outside Ayr is Alloway, the mecca of Burnsiana. As well as the cottage, there is the Land O' Burns Centre, an ugly purpose-built construction with a good tearoom and copious quantities of Burns coasters and tins of shortbread for sale inside. Over the road, however, is the genuinely eerie ruin of Alloway Kirk, the scene of the witches' dance in Burns' narrative poem *Tam O'Shanter* and the tiny, atmospheric site of Burns' father's grave. You can follow the route of Tam, hopefully unmolested by the forces of evil, from the Kirk down to the Brig O' Doon, the fine cobble-stone bridge where Tam narrowly escaped the pursuing witches at the cost of his horse Meg's tail. Looming above the bridge is the Burns Monument, a huge, somewhat inappropriate neo-classical rotunda, which sits obtrusively in otherwise amiably small and neat gardens.

When you leave Alloway driving southwards, the sweeping, swooping B7024 carries you over the expansive Ayrshire countryside, a terrain like a rumpled sheet. Clusters of harled cottages, ranging in colour from milky white to double cream, and fields of cows confirm the appealing stereotypical Ayrshire image.

West of Maybole is the National Trust for Scotland's most popular property, Culzean Castle and Country Park, designed by Robert Adam in the late 18th century. This castellated edifice, impressively large and the height of stateliness, is welded to rocky cliffs which rise from the seething waters of the lower Firth of Clyde. From a vantage point on the battlements, the isle of Arran, and the long finger of Kintyre beyond it, ride on the horizon.

The grounds of Culzean, the first of Scotland's country parks, are lush with woodland and rhododendrons. The Visitor Centre, undoubtedly one of Scotland's most glamorous, resides in the dark, honey sandstone of Culzean Home Farm. Families come here by the busload to spend the day strolling along prepared paths, picnicking and participating in Fun Days, the Festival of Flowers, and the Music and Children's Weeks.

South of Culzean, the A77 hugs the coast from Turnberry to Stranraer, the launching point for ferries to Northern Ireland. From the A77, you can observe the abrupt parallel stripes of white mobile homes, their picture windows determinedly staring at the sea views from small bays along the coast. On a winter's day the chill grey of the sea leaks into the sky, while in the summer, the prospect of blue is more hopeful. The seashore changes gradually. Tawny sand gives way to low, black, rocky outcrops, with occasional hiccups of gravel, before arriving at the grubby tone of Girvan's beach which Edwin Muir likened to 'a huge bed that has been slept on for a long time without the sheets being changed.' Nor was the writer greatly impressed by the town itself which he described as, 'a bleak little place, unlike most Scottish sea resorts'. Muir's unkindness is a little unfair: Girvan shares with Ayr and many other British seaside towns, the strange, tired charm of a place which partied in its heyday and has not been asked to dance since, despite the adornments of cafes, amusement arcades and strings of coloured lightbulbs. Girvan's russet sandstone centre does have a more conventional visual appeal and of course the town has the touristic advantage of Ailsa Craig, the granite lump famous for its curling stones, which is moored offshore. From Girvan day-trippers are shipped out towards the vertical cliffs of this apparently unassailable island, in silhouette the shape of a well-risen fruitcake.

Fifty-odd miles from Ayr, the ferries for Northern Ireland shelter at Cairnryan and Stranraer in the deep scoop of Loch Ryan. Stranraer combines its role as port with that of market town and holiday resort. It has an active, cosmopolitan feel – petrol-station shelves are filled with maps of Ireland, cars and lorries file into town all year, and freight containers and the paraphernalia of shipping are piled inside the harbour fences. At night, the orange glow of the port's sodium lights keeps things alive, while rows of sleeping coaches give some idea of the volume of Stranraer's traffic. The town is a popular touring base for the Rinns of Galloway, the Machars and the wonderful nooks and crannies of the south-facing Solway Firth coastline.

Whithorn, the 4th-century springboard for Christianity in Scotland, is the magnet which draws visitors to the Machars, a tongue of land with Luce Bay on one side and Wigtown Bay on the other. St Ninian brought faith to the heathens nearly sixteen hundred years ago and now the faithful and the curious alike come to look at the Christian totems of the area. After an ironic glance at St John's Garage, a modern church conversion, sightseers are drawn through the garish Pend, a 17th-century archway with details of royal pilgrims writ large in paint upon it. Then comes the archaeological dig, criss-crossed with gravel paths and string markers, beyond which the ancient priory lies.

On the tip of the Machars promontory is the one-time Isle of Whithorn. The sandbags slumped around the village in winter indicate its vulnerability: the raging Irish sea is careless of the picturesqueness of this settlement.

Across Wigtown Bay, Gatehouse of Fleet, a planned Georgian town, is a paragon of civic pride. Not a pebble out of place, it is a model of neatness, its houses, streets and harbour all impeccably kept. Kirkcudbright is its twin – buildings are crisp in pastel paint, with precise contrasting trims, and shops with traditional fronts are boutiquey. McLellan's Castle, a roofless fortified house, is Kirkcudbright's centrepiece. This coastline has long been a popular haunt with artists, and the Solway towns, reminiscent of Cornish fishing villages, are dotted with art galleries and jewellery workshops.

Rockcliffe, hiding like Kirkcudbright and Gatehouse of Fleet up an estuary, is licked, as they are, by the infamous mud of the Solway Firth. The tidal flats, streaked with silver when the sun catches the pools of water abandoned by the sea, have not always been appreciated. The transition from 'a world of waters' to 'a world of squelch' confirms that the unique scenic appeal of this particular mud has escaped many commentators.

The land girdling the southern rim of the Uplands is unlike any other part of Scotland. A comparatively mild climate is the benevolent guardian of mellow woodland, rambling hills, stubbly gorse bushes and fields which creep down to the mud flats.

En route to Dumfries, the twisty, roller-coaster A710 splices New Abbey, passing by the white-washed cornmill, the Monks' Fish Pond and Sweetheart Abbey, dramatic in its Gothic angularity and famed for the lovelorn story of its founder. Devorguilla de Balliol established the abbey in 1273 in memory of her dead husband whose embalmed heart she kept in an ivory casket. It and she were buried herein 1289.

A dozen miles further on and you enter Dumfries, the southern gateway to the area. On the Burns front, there is much to choose from: the house where he died (so disdained by Dorothy Wordsworth), the pub which was his 'favourite howff' and in which he had 'many a merry squeeze', and his mausoleum. The latter, picked out in blinding white and blue paint, was decidedly not to Keats' taste either. It is glazed and on each 25 January (the anniversary of the poet's birth), pilgrims can see the flower wreaths from the Dumfries Burns Club and the District Council of Nithsdale which render the immodest monument even more like a miniature hothouse.

In a converted 18th-century mill on the far side of the River Nith from the main body of the town resides yet another Robert Burns Centre. Upstream from the riverside centre is the Old Bridge and the wide stretch of the town's weir. In summer, couples lean into the railing on opposite banks of the river to watch the steady curtain of water and the blithely floating swans.

Dumfries itself is that common cocktail: handsome old buildings mixed and stirred with the habits of modern living. Rising from the middle of the pedestrianised shopping precinct is the enduring cone of Midsteeple. From here, Robert Burns' body was carried in ceremony to its grave in St Michael's Church. Now, tacked onto the rear of the building are an Olde Curio Shoppe, a fish-and-chicken bar and a shoe-repair shop. The precinct, once filled with the grief of 10,000 mourners, is all benches and bollards, bins and bus shelters. These black and gold fittings, the uniform of every town centre revamped for tourist tastes, are matched by signposts, pointing the well-trodden way to pit-stops along the Burns Heritage Trail.

New Bridge, Ayr (above)
Ceiling detail, Culzean Castle (opposite)

Robert Burns, Dumfries (left)
The Tam O'Shanter Inn, Ayr (top right)
The Brig o' Doon, Alloway (bottom right)
Burns Cottage interior, Alloway (opposite, top)
Ayr beach (opposite, bottom)

Fishing on the Firth of Clyde (top)
Dressing room, The Gaiety Theatre, Ayr (bottom)
Culzean Castle (opposite)

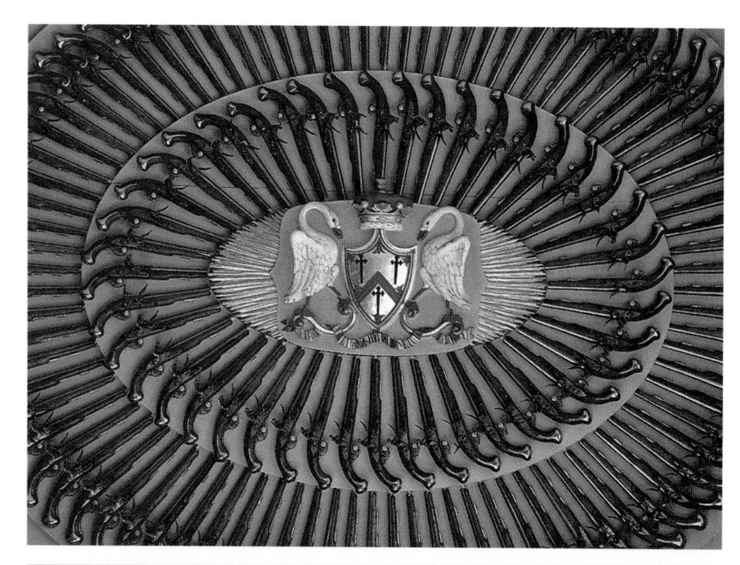

Culzean Castle (top)
Ailsa Craig (bottom)
Logan Botanic Gardens, Port Logan (opposite, top)
The Bruce Memorial, Loch Trool (opposite, bottom)

IN LOYAL REMEMBRANCE
OF
ROBERT THE BRUCE,
KING OF SCOTS,
WHOSE VICTORY IN THIS
GLEN OVER AN ENGLISH
FORCE IN MARCH, 1307,
OPENED THE CAMPAIGN OF
INDEPENDENCE WHICH HE
BROUGHT TO A DECISIVE
CLOSE AT BANNOCKBURN
ON 24TH JUNE, 1314.

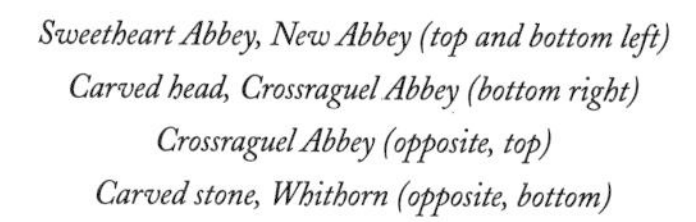

Sweetheart Abbey, New Abbey (top and bottom left)
Carved head, Crossraguel Abbey (bottom right)
Crossraguel Abbey (opposite, top)
Carved stone, Whithorn (opposite, bottom)

Bowlers, New Abbey (top)
Mill, New Abbey (bottom)
Henry Moore sculpture, Shawhead (opposite, top)
Barbara Hepworth sculpture, Shawhead (opposite, bottom)

Archaeological dig, Whithorn (above)
Statue, Kirkcudbright (opposite, top)
The harbour, Kirkcudbright (opposite, bottom)

Burns mausoleum, St Michael's churchyard, Dumfries (above)
The Globe Inn, Dumfries (below)
The Old Bridge, Dumfries (opposite)

Ravenscraig steelworks, Motherwell

The Central Lowlands

The urban waistline of Scotland, hauled in tight by the belt of the M8, comes as something of a surprise to travellers moving northwards. The ample hill ranges of the Borders suddenly give way to a rather featureless landscape which is at worst ravaged and poisoned by the workings of heavy industry and is at best criss-crossed with electricity pylons. The Central Lowlands are densely populated – the majority of Scotland's people live in and around the triangle made by Stirling, Glasgow and Edinburgh.

Between Edinburgh and Glasgow, cities so different in physical and social character that it is hard to understand why they are often discussed in the same breath, lies the heartland of Scotland's industrial past. The Central Belt represents the changing face of Scotland more visibly and more pertinently than anywhere else in the country. Here, the slow death of traditional heavy industries around which communities grew – coal mining, steel smelting, textiles weaving, ship building, freight carrying – has necessitated a reconstruction, often equally slow, built around younger industries like 'high tech' developments and tourism.

Where this facelift has taken place, it has led to some examples of preservation (as the cult of industrial heritage pulls tourists to mines and mills), some cleaning and sweeping (as Glasgow's and Edinburgh's sandstone buildings are scrubbed free of Victorian soot), some losses and some new beginnings.

Tourism, a major contributor to Scotland's purse, figures prominently in many of the changes. There is no doubt that its importance will grow, as Scotland takes its place on the European stage of economic integration and also becomes more accessible to transatlantic visitors via Glasgow Airport, which was given gateway status in 1990.

Edinburgh, with the inherent attractiveness of its geographical layout, has long been a port of call for holiday-makers and weekend-breakers. It is a city that has never required much marketing. As the home of the Scottish Enlightenment and Georgian architecture, as the sometime home to countless literary figures (among them Sir Arthur Conan Doyle, Robert Louis Stevenson, Thomas De Quincey, Sir Compton Mackenzie, Rebecca West, Norman MacCaig, and Muriel Spark), as the home to the world's largest arts festival and as the capital of Scotland, Edinburgh can simply sit and wait for admirers to arrive. They come in trickles in the spring, en masse in the summer, before leaving the city and its inhabitants to take breath as the dust of tramping sightseers' feet settles in the autumn. The 19th-century poet Alexander Smith summed up what millions have perceived: 'Hill, crag, castle, rock, blue stretch of sea, the picturesque ridge of the Old Town, the squares and terraces of the New – these things seen once are not to be forgotten.'

Early travellers trawled around the standard Edinburgh Old Town sights just as they do today, the Palace of Holyrood House and the Castle being prime targets. Thomas Pennant in 1769 marvelled at the shoulder-to-shoulder houses of the Royal Mile, squeezing as near to the Castle as they could, he thought, 'on the principle of security'. Pennant was shown the spot in Holyrood Palace, marked with a blot of blood and pointed out by tour guides still, where Mary, Queen of Scots' favourite secretary, David Rizzio, was murdered.

Within the walls which meld into the lofty rocky outcrop, Edinburgh Castle contains the Crown Room, military museums, the minuscule 11th century St Margaret's Chapel, the birthplace of James VI (later James I of England), and a handkerchief of green turf where military canine mascots lie buried. The annual Edinburgh Military Tattoo is staged on the Castle Esplanade, which is transformed in the summer from a car park into endless tiers of seating.

The wynds and closes of the Old Town prove the perfect location for organised night-time walks of horror, murder and mischief. In the shadow of jutting houses and stone stairwells, guides describe Edinburgh's seamy side for the delectation of visitors – the nocturnal activities of the murderers Burke and Hare, the burning of witches, the dark doings of split-personality Deacon Brodie (on whom Robert Louis Stevenson modelled the main character in *The Strange Case of Dr Jekyll and Mr Hyde*) and the public hangings which took place in the Grassmarket.

North of the spine along upon which the Old Town is built and north of Princes Street Gardens is Edinburgh's meticulously planned, grid-iron New Town, where Princes Street, George Street and Queen Street are the principal thoroughfares. Designed by James Craig in 1767, the New Town buildings are exemplary in their perfect if frigid Georgian symmetry and are matched only by the softer counterpart of Bath in completeness.

Surrounding the Old and New Towns are onetime villages – Swanston, Stockbridge, Colinton, Juniper Green, the Dean Village and others – whose boundaries are now smudged although their identities manage to survive under the city's municipal umbrella.

Further out, perched up above the woodland of Roslin Glen lies Rosslyn Chapel – a miniature Gothic cathedral, with small flying buttresses and immaculately carved stonework. Beside it hunch cottages, stamped with a plaque which explains that they were once an inn where King Edward VII and such literary luminaries as the Wordsworths, Sir Walter Scott, Dr Johnson and Boswell paused for refreshment as they visited the chapel.

To the northwest of Edinburgh are the bridges which span the Firth of Forth. The railway-carrying Forth Bridge, illuminated to commemorate its centenary in 1990, has an eerie beauty of its own when the wraiths of the sea haar creep in and the bridge's arches rise out of the insinuating fog like the humps of the Loch Ness Monster. Its more youthful road counterpart is itself a feat of modern engineering, albeit the cause of a debt that Scotland may never pay off.

South Queensferry looks up at the bridges from its position at the edge of the Forth; a passenger boat leaves from the pier here for Inchcolm Island where St Colm's Abbey was used in the Edinburgh Festivals of 1988 and 1989 as the gusty, rain-sliced setting for an abbreviated but convincing *Macbeth*.

West of the bridges and Inchcolm, the Forth holds its width before tapering in at Kincardine en route for Stirling. It passes Bo'ness, an unassuming town destined to become a popular commuting zone for Edinburgh and celebrated for its steam railway. Almost lost amongst timber merchants, an ironworks and some run-down warehouses, the station has a timeless quality: small boys escape from dreich grey housing estates to loiter around it, flinging stones into the nearby dock and gawping at the steam engine.

Much of the area around this shore supplies workers to Grangemouth, the oil refinery which pumps oil to Hound Point below the Forth Bridge where huge tankers lumber in from the North Sea to collect it. The refinery belches flame and rumbles ominously. The A904, part of the so-called tourist route between Stirling and Edinburgh, splices this mind-boggling, futuristic megalopolis. Chimneys, flares, steaming stacks, smoking funnels and miles of pipes, spooling like giant intestines, add to the impression that this is the budget-busting set of a science-fiction movie.

If you abandon the dawdling A904 for the much quicker M9 route between Stirling and Edinburgh, you will see Linlithgow Palace, the birthplace of Mary, Queen of Scots, standing aloof in its remarkable setting. Surrounded by verdant parklands, it rests on a knoll above the loop of the loch. The peel – the palace's loose, protective outer skin – defends against the battalions of dog-walkers and pram-pushers, and the honking and quacking ducks and geese.

There are no such sights from the M8 which shunts vehicles between Edinburgh and Glasgow. Sometimes criticised for being so boring that it sends drivers to sleep, this busy motorway is undergoing a degree of visual improvement with pencil-thin trees being planted on sections of its verges.

Although often condemned to positions as opposing weights at either end of the M8/A8 see-saw, Edinburgh and Glasgow are less than fifty miles apart. They have shared a common fate in that both have suffered from an abundance of clichés. In the relentless compare-and-contrast activity that goes on, Edinburgh is the cold-hearted, uppercrust city which conceals a grim, impoverished interior (the 'fur coat and nae knickers' image), while Glasgow is the rough-talking, razor-wielding thug of a city. Highclass tart and criminal yob: these are the tired myths upon which the slack-jawed and lazy construct more myths. Yet what is said of Edinburgh and Glasgow could undoubtedly be said of any city in the world – all have their finer points, all have their problems.

Drug addiction, dreary high-rise housing estates to which people were transplanted in the 1960s, high unemployment in areas which once relied on heavy industry – all are evidence of terrible social, economic and architectural failures. But Glasgow's own renaissance, culminating in its crowning as European City of Culture in 1990, gives validity to hopes for the alleviation of pockets of dereliction in the Central Belt. Towns and villages with inherent visual appeal, or with the dynamic of a major tourist attraction, will find it easier to revitalise themselves, although those built hurriedly to serve heavy industry are liable to be less fortunate without the injection of new industry.

The restored village of New Lanark is an example of successful rejuvenation. Its houses are now inhabited and the former cotton mills now contain offices and a visitor centre. The village, where the Welsh industrialist and social reformer Robert Owen conducted his social experiments, lies down beside the rural Clyde. Visitors can enjoy riverside walks or, inside the centre, be carried in carts on an audio-visual journey back to the 1780s. A small girl, an employee in Owen's mill, tells of his benefaction, his schemes to encourage workers, his school and his social philosophy. Elsewhere in the mill buildings are looms which crash into life and displays on steam engines and the textile industry.

The Clyde, cleansed and revitalised so that salmon have returned to it, is here a dancing, playful river, edged with vegetation and sparkling in the sunshine. Before long, as it heads for the Firth of Clyde, it will begin to accrue its seafaring and urban significance as it sidles through Glasgow's suburbs before splicing Scotland's largest city.

Because of the river, Glasgow became a major British gateway to the New World by the end of the 17th century. The tobacco, sugar and cotton trades brought great prosperity, as subsequently did the shipbuilding, coal and iron industries. Considered by poet John Betjeman to be 'the greatest Victorian city in the world', Glasgow enjoyed the boom-times. Next to Glasgow Cathedral (the monument to the city's roots as a centre of worship) is the Necropolis. There lavish, flamboyant memorials provide extravagant evidence of Glasgow's status as the hub of Victorian industry and affluence. Shipping magnates, bankers and merchants of every description paid handsomely for their prestigious plots and tombstones, and their carved names and trades evoke the once-feverish bustle of money-making.

However, in Glasgow as elsewhere, the Industrial Revolution brought in its wake severe social problems. Poor living and working conditions and then high unemployment led to another great Strathclyde tradition – the labour movement. Workers' rights and populist movements are still the stuff of Glasgow pride and Glasgow politics and museums such as the People's Palace embrace wholeheartedly the principle of 'for and about ordinary people'.

Other places which usually appear on the visitor's agenda are George Square, the palatial red stone Kelvingrove Art Gallery and the magpie Burrell Collection in Pollok Country Park. In George Square, Sir Walter Scott perches atop an 80-foot pedestal. The City Chambers, opened by Queen Victoria in 1888, is on the east side of the square. The building's interior is a debauch of marble, gilt, granite and alabaster – a vision of opulence run riot and a living testament to Victorian excess.

During 1990 a number of new venues were opened in the city, among them the refurbished, airy McLellan Galleries and the purpose-built Royal Concert Hall. These will continue to attract artists of international standing whose names, in typical Glasgow fashion, will stand on an equal footing with the city's home-grown talent.

Historically, Glasgow's hitherto unfashionable alumni have included a host of Victorian industrialists, social reformers and political leaders, as well as more celebrated sons like James Watt and Charles Rennie Mackintosh who is sometimes credited as being the father of modern architecture. Mackintosh's elongated, angular designs can best be seen in the Glasgow School of Art and in the Hill House, Helensburgh. The characteristically elongated style of the lettering he created was mimicked repeatedly for T-shirt logos and sundry memorabilia during 1990.

Beyond Glasgow proper, the countryside north of the Clyde rapidly becomes the rolling expanse of the Highlands, while south of the river the landscape is dominated by more industry and more urban populations. Paisley for example, is Strathclyde Region's second biggest centre where shoppers throng the pavements and orange buses covered in self-promoting slogans which read 'Your Wee Happy Bus' weave along the main street. Paisley's shawl-making heritage is on show at the local museum and art gallery.

West of Paisley and Glasgow, the M8/A8 coasts along beside the ever-widening estuary, passing the remnants of ship-building days. Cranes idle around the docks at Port Glasgow in Inverclyde District, home of the shipyards of Ferguson's and Scott Lithgow. Derelict Victorian warehouses and the square pillars of high-rise flats seem hopeless in contrast to the Clyde which increasingly looks like, and increasingly is, a jaunty playground for trippers and weekend sailors. Against a blue sky, with clouds sprawling on the hilltops above, tugs and ferries promenade the estuary. The Clyde seems tame and reflective, an appropriate setting for the West

Highland adventures of the puffer *The Vital Spark* in Neil Munro's book *Para Handy*.

At Gourock, the Clyde is speckled with orange, white and yellow buoys. Ferries leave from here for Dunoon and the enticing horizon of hills to the north and west. Opposite, you can see the watery creases of Loch Long and the Gare Loch, a fringe of white houses, and the Holy Loch, the former parking lot for American nuclear submarines.

Inverkip, Kip Marina and Wemyss Bay are the seaside preface to Glasgow's resort supreme, Largs. Ice-cream kiosks, a seafront full of hotels and guest-houses, emerald green park benches and the ferry terminal for the lush isle of Great Cumbrae attract trippers from Glasgow. Others visit just to taste the award-winning ice-cream and pastries of Nardini's Café, all wicker chairs and tables, children in pushchairs and knickerbocker glories.

The northern bank of the Clyde is without the homey, much-loved, well-worn atmosphere of Largs but has many compensations; its flavour is more Highland, more scenic and more dramatic. The attractive beacon of Dumbarton Rock, a volcanic plug of basalt upon which perches the remains of Dumbarton Castle, is visible for miles and dominates the skyline. Further west, the Highland fault line runs through sedate and well-heeled Helensburgh. Here large houses hold their ground on the slope above the town, hob-nobbing with Mackintosh's Hill House, its principal tourist magnet. Up over this gradation you look down on spectacular Loch Lomond, the island-dotted inspiration for the song which has made it Scotland's most famous loch.

Hill House, Helensburgh

Edinburgh terrace (top)
Princes Street Gardens, Edinburgh (bottom)
Kelvingrove Park, Glasgow (opposite, top)
City Chambers, Glasgow (opposite, bottom)

City Hall detail, Glasgow (opposite, top)
'Mercury', Merchant City, Glasgow (opposite, centre left)
City Chambers, Glasgow (opposite, centre right)
The Tenement House museum, Glasgow (opposite, bottom)
Multistorey flats, Glasgow (below)

Standing guard at Edinburgh Castle (top left)
Princes Street, Edinburgh (top right)
Festival-goers, The Mound, Edinburgh (bottom)
Festival Fringe performer, The Mound, Edinburgh (opposite, top)
Remembrance Day parade, High St, Edinburgh (opposite, bottom)

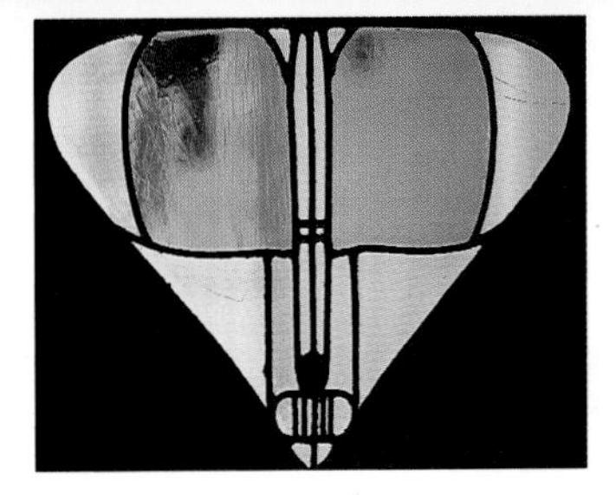

Door details, Glasgow School of Art (top and bottom)
Mackintosh furniture collection, Glasgow School of Art (centre)
The library, Glasgow School of Art (opposite)

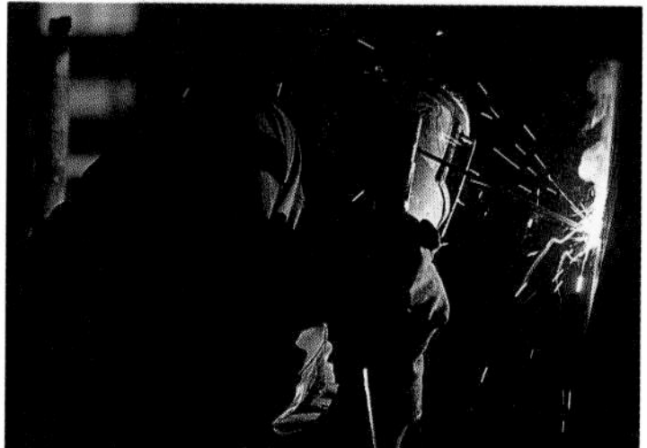

Port Glasgow docks (top)
Yarrow's shipyard, Glasgow (bottom left)
Welder, Yarrow's shipyard, Glasgow (bottom right)
Port Glasgow docks (opposite)

CK
Brayne

The Barras Market, Glasgow (above and opposite, top)
Edinburgh faces (below)
Edinburgh Tattoo (opposite, bottom)

LINGERIE & PANTY HOSE
1/2 PRICE SALE
KNICKERS DOWN 2 for £1

Guard geese, Ballantyne's whisky distillery, Dumbarton (top)
View across the Firth of Clyde from Dunoon (bottom)

Kyles of Bute (top)
Rothesay (bottom left and right

Sound of Sleat

The West

On a calm day, the majestic Ben Lomond stares down at its unruffled reflection in the still, clear waters of Loch Lomond, immune to the commercial paraphernalia at the southern end of the loch. Escaping the leaden city fumes of Glasgow, people travel the short twenty miles to savour the soft air of the West Highlands that curls around the loch. Here begins the drama of an ever-changing land- and waterscape, where bulky mountains are swallowed suddenly by wisps of low cloud, where lochs spume and spit in storms or where, under an untroubled blue sky, the terrain exudes a contentment which seems unassailable. Dorothy Wordsworth, still struggling around Scotland in 1803, marvelled at the prospect before her: 'What I had heard about Loch Lomond ... had given me no idea of anything like what we beheld: it was an outlandish scene ... The islands were of every possible variety of shape and surface – hilly and level, large and small, bare, rocky, pastoral or covered with wood'.

Halfway along the western side of the loch is Luss, a preserved village which is familiar to many as the setting for Scotland's soap opera 'Take The High Road'. Luss is also acclaimed as Scotland's prettiest village and it struck traveller Thomas Pennant similarly in 1769. In his journal he lists and wonders over the remarkable number of elderly inhabitants, who are, he decides, 'proofs of the uncommon healthiness of the place.'

Beyond Loch Lomond, west-coast mountains, creased and furrowed with age, seem to be clad in ancient pelts. White flashes of waterfalls streak their sides; vegetation is lush in a generously mild and over-wet climate, nurtured by the Gulf Stream; the seas and lochs are chameleon in temperament, switching from molten tar or sulky grey to sunny aquamarine in minutes. Solitary white-washed houses punctuate distant, apparently inaccessible shores, and roads have to take the long way round, looping for miles alongside lochs. Inhabited for centuries, Argyll, now part of the region of Strathclyde, also contains many prehistoric brochs, burial cairns and ritual stones.

The world that begins in earnest to the west of Loch Lomond is a watery one. The ragged, torn-paper coast comprise long fingers of land and water: Cowal, Bute and Kintyre are mimicked by Loch Long, Loch Fyne, the Sound of Jura and Loch Linnhe. Splinters of land – the Inner Hebrides – surface off-shore, almost always visible from the mainland, as they shadow one another on the horizon.

Past the head of Loch Long, where a sign urges 'Keep Argyll Tidy' despite the seaborne plastic debris that at times chokes the shore, the A83 climbs through Glen Croe, around the knobbly Cobbler, nearly 3000 feet high, to and beyond the post-ascent point called the Rest and Be Thankful. At Loch Fyne, a roadside smoke house and an oyster bar introduce a major west coast theme – fishing.

Herring was for many years the staple catch from Loch Fyne. Thomas Pennant recorded the 18th-century scene where every evening 'some hundreds of boats in a manner covered the surface of Loch Fine'. Even then, the herring could be wayward, vanishing for long periods before returning unexpectedly. Neil Munro's fictional crew of the puffer *The Vital Spark* remark on past abundance: 'The herrin' wass that thick in Loch Fyne in them days ... that sometimes you couldna' get your anchor to the ground'.

The tales of *The Vital Spark* convey the seductive, mañana flavour of life in these waters. The boat calls at most of the harbours here – Tarbert, Lochgoilhead, Campbeltown, Crarae Quay among others – surviving the rough seas 'that set her all awash like an empty herring box' and the Highland midges, as well as the shame of being overtaken by flash yachts or by the Caledonian MacBrayne ferries which still run to the islands from Kennacraig, Tayinloan, Oban and Ullapool.

The harbour of Inverary is still stocked with trawlers, although in the summer months, tourists are the more profitable catch. For Inverary, its 'living, nineteenth-century' jail museum, its turreted castle and its immaculate planned centre, are on the west-coast tour coach milk-run.

Beyond Inverary, the A83 meanders beside the pebbly foreshore of Loch Fyne, making an inland foray to Auchindrain, a museum composed of a collection of red corrugated-iron roofs and white buildings and the only communal tenancy township remaining in Scotland.

Crarae Garden is the first of several gardens on the Kintyre peninsula which are open to the public. It is joined by those at Kilmory Castle, Stonefield Castle Hotel, Carradale House and Gigha's Achamore House. Even outside these cultivated grounds, spikey palms and thickets of rhododendrons are common sights around the coast.

Lochgilphead, with its Loch Fyne-side grass apron, and Tarbert, at the head of West Loch Tarbert, are frequented by the sailing fraternity. At the latter, lobster-picking diners look out at the green-grey rocks and islets, topped with scrub and gorse, which pepper the loch's waters. Beyond Tarbert, the landscape turns agricultural, reminiscent of Ayrshire. The long haul down the Kintyre finger, past lone caravans hiding in rocky nooks, is rewarded by Campbeltown, an urban surprise in the middle of nowhere. Beinn Guilean skulks to the south of the town, which is, in spite of its isolation, busy enough to lay claim to an industrial estate, supermarkets and an airport. The mouth of Campbeltown Loch is plugged by the asymmetrical knoll of Davaar Island, once inhabited but now just grazed by sheep. Opposite lies Arran, afloat in the Firth of Clyde, while further south is the remote Mull of Kintyre.

Travelling north again the fatter tongues of dry ground bonding Kintyre to the mainland are also riven with sea lochs. Gulls, seals and crows patrol the wooded edges of Loch Caolisport and Loch Sween. Castle Sween, only accessible by single-track road from the north, is reputedly the oldest castle in Scotland. A defensive keep since the 12th century, it is now besieged by the static caravans which share its grassy plateau.

At the neck of the thin peninsula is the Crinan Canal. It was designed to cut out the tiresome circumnavigation of Kintyre, easing passage from the Sound of Jura to the Firth of Clyde via Loch Fyne. Work began in 1794, it was opened in 1801 and engineer Thomas Telford came to add the finishing touches in 1817 although it still proved too narrow for most vessels. Pleasure boats are now its regular customers, riding the fifteen locks between the tidy, tiny harbour of Crinan and Ardrishaig on Loch Gilp.

Before Oban on the A816 comes Kilmartin and its ancient sculptured stones. In the village's hillside churchyard is a collection of grave slabs, some encased in a miniature stone building and dating from 1300 while others are laid out in line in the open. Many were engraved by sculptors who lived around Loch Awe.

After Kilmartin, the hazardous road twists across a chunky peninsula which looks out at the picturesque island fragments on the eastern side of the Firth of Lorn – Seil (reached via the very hump-backed Clachan Bridge, built in 1791 and also known as the Bridge over the Atlantic), Scarba, Luing, Easdale (with its folk museum), Insh and Shuna. Other chips lie scattered amongst them, stretching navigators' nerves.

The leg-of-mutton-shaped island of Kerrera guards the harbour of Oban, the chief town of Argyll whose port is the gateway to several of the larger Western Isles. The scoop of Oban's harbour is so sheltered by Kerrera that the entrepreneur and philanthropist, John Knox, on a fact-finding mission in 1768, decreed it ideal as a naval base. Instead it has become a hotel-congested crossroads for sea and land traffic, an overnight stop for tourers. Its main oddity, which perches on one of the knolls, spines and hummocks of high ground encircling the town, is the 19th-century McCaig's Folly. A bizarre and improbable structure, it imitates Rome's Colosseum.

Other visitor attractions in the area include the former seat of Scottish kings, Dunstaffnage Castle, which sits at the mouth of Loch Etive, Ben Cruachan and its hidden hydro-electric scheme intestines, the Sealife Centre, where sea slugs, starfish, turbot, salmon and ling press themselves against the sides of large glass tanks, and Castle Stalker. The latter two lie along the A828, the road which merges with the A82 at Ballachulish.

Fort William, a popular destination despite the concrete ugliness of its post-war buildings, is also notorious for its weather and long has it been so. One Captain Burt, writing in the 1730s, noted: 'At Fort William I have heard the people talk as familiarly of a shower (as they call it) of nine or ten weeks as they would of anything else that was not out of the ordinary course.'

Ben Nevis, Britain's highest mountain, looms on the horizon above Fort William. A series of shoulders, rather than a mighty peak, the poet James Hogg, the Ettrick Shepherd, wrote that 'its uncouth bosom, huge masses of everlasting snow, and all that ranges both to the east and west, is wild and savage beyond measure'. Taking advantage of what the operators hope will be everlasting snow, Scotland's youngest ski resort, Aonach Mor, fed by Britain's first gondola lift, opened under the mountain's brooding stare in 1989.

As the capital of the West Highlands, Fort William is also on the West Highland railway line which runs from Glasgow to the end-of-the-line fishing port of Mallaig. It journeys through spectacular scenery – over the remote and desolate Rannoch Moor, then through Fort William, along Loch Eil, past the head of Loch Shiel and the Glenfinnan Monument (marking the place where Bonnie Prince Charlie raised his standard in 1745 before embarking on his abortive rebellion) on to Arisaig and Mallaig.

The unspoilt countryside around and north of Ardnamurchan Point, much of it inaccessible except on foot, is some of Scotland's most beautiful. Sleepy and ageless, for most of the year the sea lochs, coves and white sandy beaches are disturbed only by deer, walkers and seals. Edwin Muir, lamenting the arrival of summer visitors to the West Highlands nonetheless felt that 'underneath ... the old life went on unchanged, or almost unchanged, though the tourist could no more see it than he could see a dream'.

Fort William's geological importance is as the

south-west end of the Great Glen Fault Line, a diagonal strip between Fort William and Inverness which nearly severs Scotland. The chain of lochs is linked by the Caledonian Canal – a 29-lock, 60-mile short-cut between the North Sea and the Atlantic. The A82 which runs through the Great Glen is, unsurprisingly, a major tourist highway, passing as it does Spean Bridge with its Commando Monument, Fort Augustus, the flushed remains of Urquhart Castle, the deep and mysterious waters of Loch Ness, with the appended monster trappings of an exhibition centre.

Before reaching Fort William as it parallels the Highland Fault Line, the A82 sweeps through the chasm of Glencoe, where mountains proffer sheer, climber-defeating faces, mean gullies and relentlessly steep arcs. Behind the daunting facades, hidden corries host Glencoe's part-time ski area. Historically renowned for the massacre which took place in the glen in 1692, when the Earl of Argyll's soldiers enjoyed the hospitality of the local MacDonalds before murdering many of them on the orders of King William, Glencoe has a visual appeal which is high drama – grand opera in all climatic conditions and uncompromised by the passage of time.

The southern Highlands are more gentrified, tamer, less barren and often more cultivated. Many hotels subscribe willingly to the visual clichés of Sir Walter Scott and Queen Victoria's tartanised Highlands. Tartan carpets, antiqued wooden panelling and bad oil paintings of sporting scenes are stock features and the hotel walls are, as Edwin Muir observed, 'alert with the stuffed heads of deer'.

Of Perthshire's Loch Tay, Dorothy Wordsworth wrote: 'There is a uniformity in the lake which, comparing it with other lakes, made it appear tiresome'. However, it is the long, uninterrupted sweep of the same loch that provides the reflective properties which Thomas Pennant admired: 'The day was very fine and calm, the whole scene was most beautifully repeated in the water'.

At Loch Tay's western end is Killin and the rapids of the Falls of Dochart, while to the east is Kenmore, a white-washed estate village attached to Taymouth Castle and golf course. Within striking distance is the village of Fortingall, a roadside settlement boasting thatched cottages, an ancient yew tree (the oldest tree in Europe, it is claimed) and the rumoured site of Pontius Pilate's birth. Nearby, Scotland's longest and possibly loveliest glen, Glen Lyon, stretches away to its bleak, lonely loch.

In a pocket framed by the A82 and the A84 south west of Loch Tay and Loch Earn, Scotland's water skiing centre, are the Trossachs, another place of extraordinary natural beauty, reminiscent of the lush vegetation on the west coast. James Hogg puzzled over the Trossachs: 'They are indeed the most confused piece of Nature's workmanship that I ever saw, consisting of a thousand little ragged eminences all overhung with bushes'. The Trossachs have their watery playgrounds – Loch Lomond lies to the west, while Loch Katrine, Loch Voil and Loch Lubnaig are among the patches of blue in their middle. Aberfoyle and Callander ('a neat village, finely situated' wrote John Knox in 1786) are the gateways for the Trossachs, and both claim that touristically essential Highland gateway status too.

This compact area is standard fodder for day trippers from both Edinburgh and Glasgow; people come to cruise on Loch Katrine's steamer, the SS *Sir Walter Scott*, or to stand at the Balquhidder headstone of cattle drover and outlaw Rob Roy MacGregor, often portrayed as the 17th-century Scottish equivalent of Robin Hood. En route, sightseers may pause at the puddley Lake of Mentieth, Scotland's only named lake, as opposed to its many lochs. On one of its islands, accessed by ferry from the Port of Mentieth, is Inchmahome Priory, once frequented by Scottish royalty.

South of here, the land opens out into the flat terrain that is Scotland's Central Belt. Stirling Castle, welded like Edinburgh Castle onto a rocky out-

crop, has a westerly vista across plains which are agricultural or show other, less attractive signs of human domination. But to the north, the view is Highland, of the inviting bank of mountains, metamorphosed constantly by the temperamental inflections of light. Stirling's situation is an enviable one – it is far enough from and close enough to Edinburgh and Glasgow, and it can watch the dramatic swings in mood of the Highlands from the safety of its own pleasant doorstep.

The Wallace Monument, Stirling (top)
Monument to Robert Bruce, Bannockburn(bottom)
Deer stalking in the Trossachs: the hunters ... (opposite, top)
... and the hunted (opposite, bottom)

Loch Awe (top)
Loch Linnhe (bottom)
Loch Fyne (opposite, top)
Loch Creran (opposite, bottom)

Castle Sween (left)
Urquhart Castle (below)

Scone Palace (above)
Inveraray Castle (left)

REGENT HOTEL

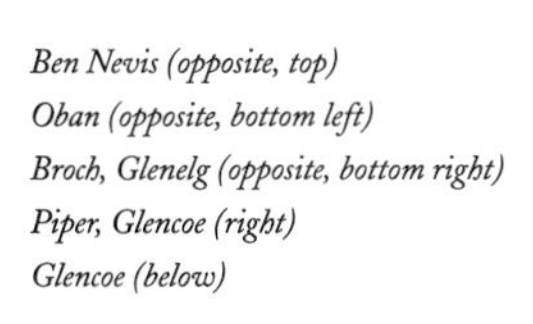

Ben Nevis (opposite, top)
Oban (opposite, bottom left)
Broch, Glenelg (opposite, bottom right)
Piper, Glencoe (right)
Glencoe (below)

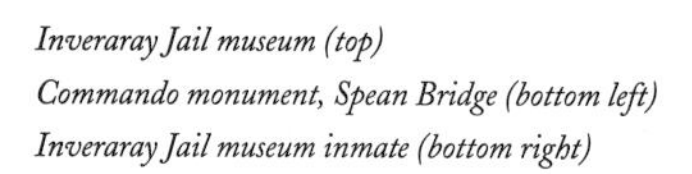

Inveraray Jail museum (top)
Commando monument, Spean Bridge (bottom left)
Inveraray Jail museum inmate (bottom right)

Glenfinnan Monument (top left)
The Sea-life Centre, Loch Creran (top centre)
Caledonian Canal, Fort Augustus (bottom)

Clan flag, Clan Macpherson Museum, Newtonmore

5

The East

The hump-back of Britain, which bulges from Inverness around the coast to Dundee and the Firth of Tay, is veined with many of Scotland's principal roads and rivers. Inverness, Aberdeen, Dundee and Perth form a quadrilateral of the North's cities, exceeded in population only by Glasgow and Edinburgh. But before the hump proper begins, there is Fife, the fold of flesh hanging above Scotland's Glasgow-Edinburgh waistline. St Andrews is the region's learned elder. The town's features – golf, the bitter North Sea wind, the oldest university in Scotland, sandstone sweetness – have appealed to sportspeople, holiday-makers, students and poets. George Bruce captured St Andrews the Venerable in his poem:

Old tales, old customs and old men's dreams
Obscure this town. Memories abound.
In the mild misted air, and in the sharp air
Toga and gown walk the pier.
The past sleeps in the stones.

Separating overhang from hump is the Firth of Tay, where the river of the same name melds with the North Sea. The Tay begins its map life as a quavery blue line in the west of Scotland. En route for Dundee, it discards names (changing from Allt-na-Lund, Coninish, Fillan and Dochart to Tay) and gets swallowed temporarily by little and large lochs (Dochart and Tay) before completing its 120-mile journey. As the longest river in Scotland, the Tay is the water-filled artery of Highland Perthshire. Characterised by its rolling hills, fertile valleys and welts of Munros (mountains over 3000 feet), the former county is now shared between two regions, Central and Tayside. Sir Walter Scott declared it 'the fairest portion of the northern kingdom'.

The Tay is one of the seams of gold in the region, mined by tourism and by those indulging in country pursuits. In season, salmon and trout fly-rods arch over the river; during the summer, flotillas of multicoloured racing rafts lumber through deep, sluggish waters; and year-round convoys of canoeists dart along the Tay, sliding round eddies and careering over rapids. This is the river's leisured, contemporary face. The remnants of the recent past also lie scattered on its banks. Abandoned, rusting cars, plastic bags, matted branches and the stubborn bulk of fallen trees comprise the occasional debris.

More attractively, rumour, tale and history are lapped by the Tay's waters too. At Aberfeldy, a typical one-street Highland town which made its literary mark in Burns' poem 'The Birks O' Aberfeldy', the river surges under a stone bridge. Built in 1733 by the English General Wade as he pushed into Scotland to put down insurrection, the celebrated bridge is just one example of Wade's surviving contribution to Scotland's infrastructure.

Dunkeld, populated like Aberfeldy by a mixture of pram-pushing locals and the green-wellied brigade, also sits beside the Tay, which is by now joined by the Tummel. Dunkeld and its medieval cathedral were at one time the spiritual centre of Scotland where St Columba reputedly established a monastery. Further along is Birnam, whose 'moving trees' make a brief, dramatic appearance in Shakespeare's *Macbeth*.

Perth, dubbed a 'Gateway to the Highlands' (as indeed is Stirling) and 'the Fair City', straddles the Tay. Sir Walter Scott rhapsodized over the city ('so eminent for the beauty of its situation'), and even today, the city receives accolades for offering the best quality of life of any British city to its residents. A renowned theatre, lush green parklands and a string of chain stores ensure the city's popularity. Regular animal sales retain Perth's links with its past as an important market town, a role which is now complemented by a whisky distillery and by a surprising density of car showrooms. The castellated mansion of Scone Palace, on the outskirts of Perth, lies on the site which was, until Perth lost its crown to Edinburgh, the ancient royal seat of Scotland.

Scotland's fourth largest city, Dundee, where the Tay sweeps into the sea, has changed its commercial clothes with unfailing regularity. Profits from trade in fish, textiles and whale blubber once filled the city's coffers. Today, marmalade, cakes and comics like publisher DC Thomson's *The Beano* and *Dandy* make their economic contribution, as does the tourist attraction ship *The Discovery*, the vessel of Antarctic explorer Captain Scott, which has found its final resting place on Dundee's waterfront. The world's best-known 'worst poet', William McGonagall, lived in Dundee and modestly dubbed himself the city's poet.

A necklace of Perthshire settlements lie along the A9, the spinal cord of north eastern Scotland and the principal route from Perth to Inverness and beyond. Pitlochry, a tourist nub of knitwear shops and tartanry, vies with Aberfeldy for the honour of being the town at the very centre of Scotland. Further on up the A9 is Aviemore, a purpose-built ski centre derided for its architectural ugliness. Sporadic promises to pull it down and start again have never materialised, but consolation for Aviemore's suburban unsightliness is quickly found in the craggy, brooding splendour of the Cairngorms, Britain's highest mountain mass.

Lying to the east of the Cairngorms, is Royal Deeside, playground of the British monarchy. Here, some of the lower, lumpy hills around the River Dee are luxuriously clothed in deciduous trees, as opposed to the regimented ranks of plantation pines which march up and down many Scottish mountains. Braemar, famed for its royal crowd-pulling Highland Gathering, did not find equal favour with Robert Louis Stevenson. Afflicted by illness in the place where he wrote *Treasure Island*, he subsequently moaned that 'my native air was more unkind than man's ingratitude.'

Cupped by hills, beside the Dee, is Ballater, a well-heeled Highland town, much advantaged by the patronage of the Windsors from nearby Balmoral. Hunting, fishing and shooting shops, the butcher's, the baker's and the newsagent's all drip with royal warrants. This is where heirs to the throne buy their Scottish sweeties (boilings to the initiated) and their pies and this is also where they try to find some peace. 'Independently of the beautiful scenery, there was a quiet, a retirement, a wildness, a liberty, and a solitude, that had such a charm for us' wrote Queen Victoria in her journal. But she wasn't confronted by the summer fleets of touring coaches which growl into Ballater and prowl around Balmoral in hope of a royal sighting.

The A93 threads these towns together, before arriving ultimately at Aberdeen, the famed granite city. Novelist Lewis Grassic Gibbon described life in Aberdeen as comparable to 'passing one's existence in a refrigerator'. Aberdeen's granite has provoked frosty shudders ('a grey glimmer like a morning North Sea, a cold steeliness that chills the heart' continued Gibbon) and admiration. The city's champions prefer to dwell on Aberdeen's lighter, beamier side – the twinkling silver mica in the dour granite and the bountiful supply of roses which nod from every roundabout and central reservation. A large, sprawling conurbation, Aberdeen has grown wealthy from mining the sea – firstly for its fish and, more recently, for its oil.

Big multinationals have brought money and box-like modern office buildings to the city, as well as a decidedly cosmopolitan, 'something happening' air. Watercolour skies, spires and towers, the night-time orange glow of docked ships' lights and sandy beaches are some of Aberdeen's pleasures, undiminished by the satellite dishes which blister buildings or by the tower blocks which look wistfully out to sea.

The coast north and south of Aberdeen is pitted with coves, fishing villages and towns, some disused, others, like Peterhead, still busy. There is gawky ugliness – the town centre of Fraserburgh appears to be built around its public toilets and lumpen modern flats squat on its outskirts – and there is infinite charm. Portsoy is a sleepy, ex-fishing village near Banff, thought to be the oldest harbour on the Moray Firth coast. Its harbour arms clasp only a few bobbing fish-for-supper boats now, and old men gather beside the water to chat, sun themselves and to watch for visitors.

Peterhead is dominated by its fishing industry. Trawlers are tightly packed, like cattle standing flank to flank in a pen; cranes stretch into the skyline; the prison inhabits the righthand prong of the harbour and a housing estate is penned in by a wire fence taller than that of the prison. The one-time spa town earned its living from whales, then herring and now white fish. The profits of oil have spilled into Peterhead too, and it remains the busiest fishing port in Europe.

Under the jutting wedge of the non-island Black Isle is Inverness, booming stone-built capital of the Highlands and tourist magnet. Guest houses galore accommodate the visitors who come in search of Nessie at Loch Ness, or travel to pay their respects at the eerily silent battlefield of Culloden. At Loch Ness, they find a visitors' centre detailing the multi-million pound searches for the monster. Suspicious ripples scuff the loch waters, and the myth is fed again. At Culloden, wind-bitten flags mark the four corners of the scrubby, heathery field which saw the bloody defeat of the Young Pretender, Charles Edward Stuart, and his supporters by the English in 1746. As you stand amidst a sprinkling of lithe silver birches, the site of the last battle fought on British soil can still send a shiver down the spine. In Inverness itself, you can buy 'I LOVE SCOTLAND' car stickers, bags and T-shirts, or you can attend a cabaret evening of Scottish folk songs and Highland dancing, where strips of tartan fabric are thumbtacked to the roof supports and elderly ladies 'ooh' when a burly fellow in a kilt comes on stage. Despite the man-made tourist attractions, the town never loses its restrained, decent Highland feel. Traditional trades have turned their hand to tourism too. Woollen mills are dotted around Inverness and a short drive into the verdant lushness of Strathspey reveals a number of whisky distilleries, usually with visitor centres. Laid-on entertainment may complement the natural appeal of the area, but the haunting, captivating landscapes of the Great Glen, as wraiths of mist rise up from the lochs, and night slides down over the mountains, are still unsurpassable.

The Tay Road Bridge, Dundee (opposite, top)
Traditional Sunday morning promenade along the pier, St Andrews (opposite, bottom)
St Andrews beach (top)
Entrance to St Andrews Golf Club (centre)
Gravestone, St Andrews (bottom)

Dunkeld Cathedral details (above)
St Monans (opposite, top)
Insh Church, near Kincraig (opposite, bottom)

Cardhu distillery, Spey Valley (opposite)
Distillery signs (top left and right)
Linn of Dee (below)

Blair Castle (above)
Balmoral Castle (below)
Fyvie Castle (opposite)

Braemar Highland Gathering

Loch Morlich (above)
The harbour, Pittenweem (below)
Pipers, Braemar Highland Gathering (opposite, top left and bottom)
The Black Watch Monument, Aberfeldy, (opposite, top right)

Blair Atholl countryside (above)
Standing stone, Clava (right)
Fortified house, Corgarff (opposite, top)
Spey Valley countryside (opposite, bottom)

Aberdeen harbour (top)
Union St, Aberdeen (bottom far left)
Marischal College, Aberdeen (above)
Royal coat-of-arms, Kings College, Aberdeen (bottom right)
Caird Hall, Dundee (opposite, top)
Inverness (opposite, bottom)

Pluscarden Abbey (above)
Strathspey steam railway, Boat of Garten (opposite)

5025
50
INVERNESS

Beinn Eighe National Nature Reserve, Ross and Cromarty

6

The North

If that characteristically soporific and heavy Highland air is partially lost to central and southern Highland villages which have been shaken awake by the commercial edge of tourism and by in-coming, refugee urbanites from Edinburgh, Glasgow and London, it is abundant north of the Great Glen. The low population figures, the absence of roads in much of Caithness and Sutherland and the survival of traditional industries have ensured that the hurried pace of modernity has little place here.

Although this is a romantic and generalised notion, it is one that has been confirmed by commentators over the centuries. In the 1930s, Edwin Muir offered his perception of the quintessential Highlands, where he found 'a sense of having a great deal of time and space to do what I liked with, a common feeling in the Highlands'. In 1769, Thomas Pennant remarked on the perhaps clichéd but admirably relaxed laissez-faire attitude of the Highlands and Highlanders. He was rather blunt: 'the manners of the native Highlander may justly be expressed in these words: indolent to a high degree, unless roused to war, or to any animating amusement ... hospitable to the highest degree, and full of generosity'.

Just how little has changed is reflected in the economic structure of the north. Fishing, the staple industry for hundreds of years, remains crucial to the settlements on the coastal fringes of what remains largely inaccessible terrain. What John Knox wrote while surveying the north for investment potential in 1786, is still true: 'Mountains, rocks, and moss compose the greatest part of these counties but Nature has made ample amends for the poverty of the soil, in the great abundance of fish that are found on or near the eastern as well as the western shores of this division of our island.'

And so fishing villages survive, slightly jaded in comparison with their herring-based boom days, but surviving nonetheless, assisted by summer visitors who come to enjoy uncongested beaches and to relish the balmy air which savours of the past.

Beyond the Black Isle, the A9, one of the few roads in the north with two carriageways, continues on its journey, tracing the coastline all the way to John o'Groats. It sidesteps Dornoch, a popular golfing and family holiday resort with a squat unpretentious cathedral, and passes Dunrobin Castle, the ancient seat of the Earls of Sutherland where the public can now view a lavish interior and gardens modelled on those at Versailles.

The road winds on around the coast, sometimes clinging to cliff tops, and sometimes traversing agricultural tracts. At Helmsdale, visitors are tempted up the single track A897 to pan for gold, which inevitably proves elusive amidst the gravelly river banks, crabbit alders, sheep and crofts scored out on the land with wooden fence posts.

Back on the A9, a sign reading 'Caithness Spring Water Bottled Here' points out one contemporary industry. Touristic diversions include a llama farm and small fishing harbours like Latheron's, where a net-strewn nook encircles the lone rocky obelisk, a scaled-down harbinger of the Duncansby Head stacks to come. The attractions of this eastern coast are obvious – crescents and long bands of pale mandarin sand contrast with the brown and green hills which stop short in their tracks before sheering into the North Sea. However, the ruins of croft houses, neglected in favour of pre-fabricated, double-glazed modern homes, gall eyes which search for history preserved rather than the faceless signals of the late 20th century.

The shore around Wick (its name a corrupted version of the Norse word 'vik', meaning a bay) is garnished with layered rocks like wafer biscuits. Encircling the town's trawlers is a harbourside of fish-and-chip shops, and the grey corrugated iron of Simpson's Ice Factory. Wick itself is just as Thomas Pennant's abrupt 18th-century description has it: 'a small borough town with some good houses'. It also has an airport, the vast sweep of sand of Sinclair's Bay nearby and the holiday role of being a touring base for the area contained within the road triangle of the A9, the A836 and the A882.

Caught in the net of this triangle is the scattering of houses, novelty shops and the tiny industrial estate which comprise John o'Groats, famous for being mainland Britain's most northerly point even though it is not. From John o'Groats, a minor road leads to Duncansby Head, sometimes lauded as Scotland's answer to the Grand Canyon. The well-worn paths across the cliff-top draw walkers to views of chasms and gashes in the cliff face, where the sea boils below and seabirds bicker overhead. Giant fingers rising up from the ocean floor, the stacks are monumental, sculptures chiselled by the elements.

Before Thurso, which completes the triangle, comes the Castle of Mey, the Queen Mother's tall, angular occasional home. Next is Dunnet Head, the true most northerly point of the British mainland. A peat-boggy knobble of a peninsula, the 400-foot top of Dunnet Head provides panoramic views of the Orkney islands and the irascible, life-taking Pentland Firth.

Castletown, between Dunnet and Thurso, was where the Caithness flagstone industry was founded in 1842. The village was purpose-built to house the quarrying workers, the result of whose efforts paved cities all over Britain. Although the industry collapsed after the introduction of concrete-cast slabs, fields around Caithness are still edged by walls made of vertically dug-in flagstones.

Thurso is a town which catches visitors unawares. Biggish, with a full complement of professionals ranging from lawyers to architects, Thurso is an urban outpost. It sports a cosmopolitan air, primarily because it is an employee-feeder town for the invidiously baby-blue globe and outbuildings of Dounreay nuclear power station. However, the economic advantage of local employment provided by the station is soured by the unusually high incidence of leukaemia and other cancers in this vicinity, although the nuclear industry denies that these can be attributed to the Dounreay complex.

Threading the towns and villages of the north coast together is the A836, the only west–east link for over thirty miles. The few roads that run north–south are, with the exception of the coastal routes, classified as narrow with passing places. This undeveloped infrastructure has protected the unique northern interior, sometimes tagged as Europe's last great wilderness. Included in this description is the Flow Country which, claim its vociferous and persuasive environmentalist champions, has been threatened in recent years by commercial operations like afforestation and by an over-working of the peat bogs.

The landscape, now a definite magnet for visitors and an economic benefit, was once decreed economically hopeless. Of Sutherland's hunched primeval sandstone mountains, the smooth-edged lochs and miles of wilderness, John Knox wrote: 'it is composed of mountains of rock and strata, extensive morasses and impassable bogs ... (it) must unavoidably remain an inhospitable, sterile desert, to the end of time'.

At Durness, Knox was relieved to discover more fertile terrain. Today, visitors to the town marvel at the cathedral dimensions of the limestone Smoo Cave, or they ride the Kyle of Durness ferry to Cape Wrath, summed up with peculiar effectiveness in the unflowery prose of Knox as 'a coast of perpendicular rock, and the dread of mariners'.

At Durness, the road turns south towards Kinlochbervie and its two harbours, and to Laxford Bridge, where Prince Charles goes salmon-fishing as the guest of the Duke of Westminster. Moored offshore is the island of Handa, the high-cliffed sanctuary for seabirds. Boat excursions operate from Scourie to the once-inhabited island which was deserted after the potato famine of 1845.

Between Scourie and Ullapool are bays freckled with islands, innumerable sealochs and fresh water lochs and the strange, intriguing shapes of mountains like Quinag (2653 feet), Suilven (2399 feet) which forms the dramatic backcloth for the busy fishing and holiday village of Lochinver, Canisp (2779 feet) and Stac Polly (2009 feet).

You descend into Ullapool from both north and south on the A835. Residing near the mouth of the sliver of Loch Broom, Ullapool was established in 1788 by the British Fishery Society, when the pier, an inn and storehouses were erected. Its smell is heavily briney, and its streets, laid out in a grid-iron and with Gaelic names, are still frequented by fishermen, often from Norway, or from eastern Europe and further afield. Out on Loch Broom, large factory ships, 'klondikers' as they are known locally, rest at ease, keeping their distance from the trawlers which cluster in the harbour and from the ferries which sail across the Minch to Stornoway.

The wide sea opening which shrinks to become Little Loch Broom and Loch Broom is speckled with the Summer Isles, the collective name for Tanera Mor, Tanera Beg, Isle Ristol, Glas-leac Mor and Glas-leac Beag. Also in the broad inlet are Priest Island, Bottle Island and Horse Island, while further south is Gruinard Island, still marked as a danger zone on many maps. This island, a benign-looking tawny and green bump in Gruinard Bay, was the site chosen for the testing of chemical weapons during the Second World War, and was defiled and poisoned by lethal anthrax spores for decades after the war. Although it was given a clean bill of health in the late 1980s, many continue to be wary. In the context of Gruinard Bay, unspoilt and blithe on a sunny day, it proves hard to contemplate the murderous intentions of mankind.

In the next bay, Loch Ewe, a Royal Navy fuel depot laced with barbed wire, continues the deadly theme. In welcome contrast, human endeavour comes to the fore at Inverewe Gardens. In 1862, Osgood Mackenzie began the laborious task of coaxing exotic plant life out of a desolate promontory. Today, the lush vegetation of a 'cool temperate' variety is a credit to his efforts. Such features as a Japanese Peace Garden are fed by the Gulf Stream and are nurtured by National Trust for Scotland gardeners.

Pouring into Loch Ewe is the outlet of Loch Maree, often acclaimed as Scotland's most beautiful loch. Vehicular access to Loch Maree is by its southern shore, either travelling from Gairloch or Kinlochewe, where the factors contributing to Loch Maree's reputation are self-evident. It offers a unique combination: a cluster of tree-covered islands, the scenic allure of the Victoria Falls, mountains like the pointy Slioch (3217 feet), the ancient remains of the Caledonian forest and the proximity of the looming, strange red sandstone Torridon peaks.

South of Loch Maree lies the Ben Eighe National Nature Reserve, an estate of 11,000 acres which was the first national nature reserve to be declared in Britain. It is named after the seven mile-long summit ridge which in turn borders the north-east edge of the Torridon Estate. Owned since 1967 by the National Trust for Scotland, this estate contains the Torridon mountains, glowing redly, capped with white quartzite, and estimated to be over 750 million years old.

The Torridons are bounded by a rough quadrilateral of roads, all of which carefully circumnavigate the mountains. The driving terrain is nonetheless far from easy – roads are single-track and slow, and cars grind up tortuous hills or plough through long glens. At Glen Carron, the A890 parallels the railway line. Mustard yellow British Rail trucks beetle along the glen, striking out for their depot near Stromeferry, a point on the line to the Kyle of Lochalsh.

For those who drive in from the east on the A87, passing the Five Sisters of Kintail, mountainous Siamese quintuplets joined together at the shoulder, or for those who come from the north, the Kyle of Lochalsh is a staging post, a watering hole for travellers who pause on the mainland before making the tiny leap over the sea to Skye.

OPEN
FIRST & LAST
FIRST & LAST
SCOTLAND
JOHN O'GROATS

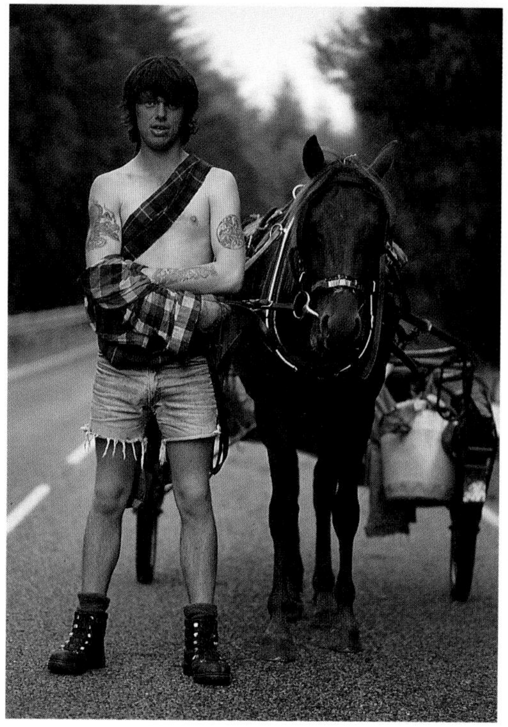

"JESUS" IS COMING SOON

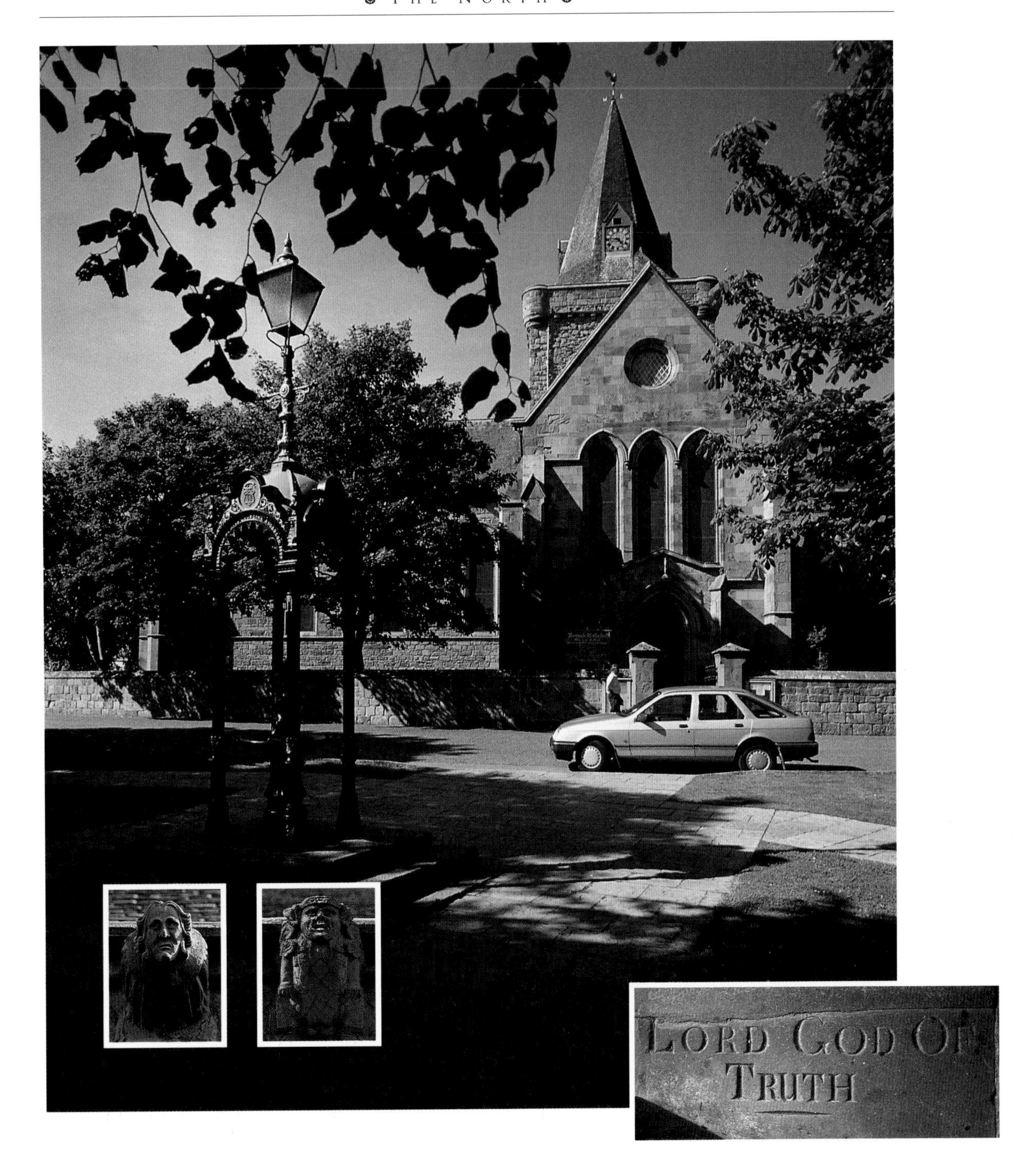

Dornoch Cathedral (above)
John o' Groats (opposite, top)

Dunrobin Castle

Scarfskerry (top)
Caithness farmers (bottom)
Dounreay nuclear reactor (opposite, top)
Duncansby Stacks (opposite, bottom)

Plockton (above)
Handa (left)

Klondikers, Ullapool (above)
The harbour, Lochinver (right)

Ullapool (above)
Unloading the catch, Lochinver (left)

Sea campion, Isle of May (top left)
Primula Scotica (top centre)
Road sign (top right)
Curlew (centre)
Inverewe gardens, Poolewe (bottom and opposite)

Roadside piper (top left)
Weaver, Lochcarron (top right)
War memorial, Glen Shiel (bottom)

Loch Maree (top)
Small loch, near Scourie (bottom)

Resident, Rubha Ardvule, South Uist

The Hebrides

When Dr Samuel Johnson first set foot on Skye in September 1773, he was, as people usually are, enamoured of the idea of islands. Escape from the mainland seemed a romantic notion – his journey to the Hebrides with James Boswell, his Scottish companion and amenuensis, had been talked of for 10 years and now the duo were embarked upon it. But their autumn tour was to be far from ideal. Frustrated by inclement weather, their onward boat trip from Skye was repeatedly postponed and Boswell grew impatient. Demonstrating uncharacteristic ambivalence, Johnson ticked him off for his haste: 'Sir, when a man retires into an island, he is to turn his thoughts entirely on another world.'

Time for contemplation, a slowing of the heartbeat which pulses through mainland life and a more mellow, gentle existence: these are the freedoms and promises held out by islands. However, Johnson's happy illusion soon wore thin when confronted with the realities of island life. Trapped by atrocious weather first on Skye, then Raasay, then Coll and lastly on Mull, the pair found that the islands represented a sea-strangled prison, not freedom at all. Forgetful of his earlier pleasure at the prospect of island living, Johnson said in despair: 'I want to be on the main land, and go on with existence. This is a waste of life'.

Like Johnson and Boswell, the initial impressions of visitors to any one island will invariably revolve around preconceptions about island life and around the hauntingly remote land- and seascapes. Accumulating knowledge, travellers who traverse a number of islands, whether in the Inner or Outer Hebrides, will next find the visual and geographical variety of the islands striking. Some, like Skye, Harris and Rhum are jagged with mountain ridges. Others, like Tiree, North Uist and Benbecula are almost completely flat. As in the cases of Harris and South Uist, the craggy, inhospitable cliff-faces on the eastern seaboards smooth out to become flat, sandy machair land on their Atlantic western coasts. As well as the named or inhabited islands, there are archipelagos of islets and reefs, bare and barren, or just abandoned. Some loom out of the mist, high ridges, sullen lumps and bulbous mounds, while many scarcely break the surface of the sea, floating like the piebald backs of basking whales.

These are the most familiar images, mere snapshots of islands which stand for considerably more. When John Knox was touring the Hebrides in 1786, he wrote: 'The face of the country, the produce by sea and land, the language, manners, and dress of the people, are similar in those respects to the opposite coast of the Highlands; but the timber is nearly exhausted.' While the cultural life of the

Highlands – Gaelic and the power of the church are notable examples – is vulnerable on the mainland to other influences and has been eroded over the years, the Hebrides have managed to preserve that culture largely intact.

Gaelic is the first and sometimes the only language of islanders. The further west you go, the more this is confirmed. On Skye, roadsigns are in Gaelic and English. On Lewis, to make a strong political point, signs are exclusively in Gaelic. As maps are usually in English, it makes travel an uphill struggle for visitors, but the argument is certainly clear: the preservation of Gaelic is a far higher priority than ease of passage for tourists.

The closer to the mainland an island is, the more mainland influences can be seen, simply because of accessibility. Islay, Jura and Gigha, which all fall under Strathclyde's political administration, form the southern end of the Hebrides. Islay is busy and thriving – combining its roles as popular holiday destination and world-famous home of malt whisky distilleries. Its main town, Bowmore, accommodates visitors with teashops and cafes, and attracts cameras to the photogenic Bowmore Round Church, built in 1769 in a circular shape to deprive the Devil of corners in which to hide. Gaelic is still spoken across shop counters, but there are many incoming voices to be heard too.

Unlike Islay, Jura and Gigha are scantily populated and scantily served. Shops number no more than one or two, and inhabitants add up to hundreds rather than thousands. As a group, the three are visually unalike. Sharing some traits, Gigha and Islay hearken back to the rhododendron-clad mainland – pockets of lush vegetation accompany peat bog and moorland, while Jura is an extraordinarily desolate, undisturbed and uncultivated island. Only a five-minute ferry journey from Islay, the eight-mile drive to the first and only town, Craighouse, is a chillingly barren one across the lower flanks of the Paps of Jura. It was further along the island's only road, near the tip which looks out at the Corrievreckan Whirlpool, that George Orwell, dying slowly of tuberculosis, wrote *Nineteen Eighty Four*.

North of the tiny Oronsay and Colonsay, Coll, Tiree, Staffa, Iona and Mull comprise the next Inner Hebridean group. Mull, like Islay, is a favourite holiday resort, able to offer a range of activities and excursions to Fingal's Cave at Staffa and to the second cradle of Scottish Christianity, Iona. Mull's inherent attractiveness was noted by novelist and poet James Hogg, writing to Sir Walter Scott upon his arrival there: 'The mountains are high, the coast, except in the bay, bold and rocky... the ruins of Castle Duart stood on the point beyond us, and upon the whole, the scene was rather interesting'. Its Little Theatre, the smallest theatre in Britain, the fossil tree at Ardmeanach and the town of Tobermory (established as a fishing port in 1788, but now more often frequented by Scotland's yachting fraternity) are added tourist incentives.

From Mull, it is hire-boats that risk the choppy, bad-tempered waters to get to Staffa and peer at Fingal's Cave, graphically described by Sir Walter Scott: 'The stupendous columnar side walls – the depth and strength of the ocean with which the cavern is filled – the variety of tints formed by stalactites dropping and petrifying between the pillars ... the corresponding variety below, where the ocean rolls over a red, and in some places a violet-coloured rock, the basis of the basaltic pillars – the dreadful noise of those august billows so well corresponding with the grandeur of the scene – are all circumstances unparalleled'. Keats was more succinct in his eulogy to the inspirational cave: 'For solemnity and grandeur, it far surpasses the finest cathedral.'

Boswell and Johnson, pummelled by equinoxial gales, were relieved to reach Iona, or Icolmkill, its Gaelic name which they used. Awed by the austere site of Columba's 6th-century Christian settlement at Port na Churaich (Port of the Coracle) and by St Oran's Chapel, built *circa* 1080, Johnson poured forth: 'We are now treading that illustrious Island, which was once the luminary of the Caledonian regions, whence savage clans and roving barbarians derived the benefits of knowledge, and the blessings of religion.'

Coll and Tiree lie to the west of the northern end of Mull. Similar in that they are both primarily flat crofting islands, Tiree with its much larger population tends to take centre-stage, not least because it often tops the British daily league of sunshine hours on television weather forecasts. Its multiple sandy beaches and wide, sweeping bays have become the venue for world-class wind-surfing competitions. Another sign of its eminently reliable, if over-boisterous, wind is the pegging-down of all moveable objects. As on many of the Outer Hebridean islands, caravans, sheds and greenhouses are staked and roped to the ground and nothing much above the height of a small bush survives the onslaught of westerly gales.

Coll was dismissed by John Knox, who was surprisingly thorough in his island-bagging: 'It is greatly inferior to Tiree in fertility, being composed mostly of rock, some blowing sand, and a very small portion of arable land.'

In the centre of the wide arc formed by Coll, Tiree, Ardnamurchan on the mainland and Skye sit the islands of Canna, Rhum, Muck and Eigg, collectively known as the Small Isles. The rough diamond of Rhum dominates in size and in scale. Once populated by over four hundred people, its mountain range and the nature trails organised by its owner, the Nature Conservancy Council, are today the home mainly of wildlife. Muck, the smallest and most southerly of the group, still has a tiny farming community, while Eigg and its sugarloaf peak, the Sgurr of Eigg, is privately-owned.

Ownership of islands is an intriguing topic. Some, like Tiree, are held by the titled families that have owned them for centuries. Others belong to bodies like the National Trust for Scotland and the Nature Conservancy Council. And a smaller number, like Gigha, appear on the property pages of national newspapers from time to time, available to the highest bidder.

Whoever the island owner, crofters' tenancies have been protected since the Croftings Holdings Act of 1886 and the vigorous crofting union is always on stand-by to campaign for the rights of its members when necessary. Crofting, like fishing, remains a stalwart industry in the islands. Before the 1886 act, in response to the forcible ejection from their crofts of the Clearances and to maltreatment by landowners, crofters had rebelled on some of the islands – beginning on Bernera in 1874 and ending on Skye in the early 1880s. In 1883, a Royal Commission was set up to investigate the crofting issue, and three years later the Crofters' Bill was introduced in the House of Commons.

It was by no means the first time that Skye, the largest Hebridean island, had found its way into Scottish history books. For the lobster-shaped Misty Isle brims with the much-romanticised tales of the Young Pretender, Charles Edward Stuart, and Flora Macdonald. In Portree, they said their last farewell before Bonnie Prince Charlie left Scottish soil forever. When Boswell and Johnson called by only 28 years later, they enjoyed Flora Macdonald's hospitality, her narration of the flight of the Prince and then bedded down in the very room where the Young Pretender had slept. Of their host, Boswell wrote a diminutive description: 'A little woman, of a genteel appearance, and uncommonly mild and well-bred'.

Boswell and Johnson also stayed at the seat of the Clan Macleod, Dunvegan Castle ('built upon a rock close to the sea') while waiting to go to Mull. Although it rained continually, they were able to see something of Skye and its 'wild, moorish, hilly, and craggy' landscape.

Today when visitors arrive by car ferry at the white-washed houses and bed-and-breakfast signs of Kyleakin, they can follow the sign towards 'Sleat, Garden of Skye' or they can continue along the A850 past the Cuillin mountains. The heaving peaks of the Black Cuillin and the rounded mounds of the Red Hills are unforgettable sights. Alexander Smith, in his 1865 book *A Summer In Skye*, expressed his continued wonder: 'Somehow these hills never weary. I never become familiar with them. Intimacy can no more stale them than it could the beauty of Cleopatra ...'

To the north of the Cuillins is Portree, Skye's pleasant fishing harbour capital and a safe yacht anchorage sheltered by two long headlands. At the far end of Skye, Uig, the departure port for ferries to the Outer Hebrides, is an unprotected bay, lashed by Atlantic swells and westerly winds. From here, boats cross the shortest stretch to Lochmaddy on North Uist or Tarbert on Harris. The sea alternatives from mainland Oban and Ullapool to Stornoway, Barra and Lochboisdale on South Uist take several hours longer.

Once called the Long Island, the 130-mile chain of Outer Hebridean islands is the last westerly bastion of human habitation before North America. The 10 populated islands contain just over 30,000 people in total, 8,000 of whom live on the island of Lewis in Stornoway, the only major town in the Western Isles and the administrative seat of the powerful Western Isles Islands Council (Comhairle nan Eilean), the well-muscled champion of Gaelic.

Lewis, and especially the area around Stornoway, drives home the conflicting desires and expectations of local people and tourists. More so here than on the other islands, the visitor who comes looking for an old and indigenous architecture will find it wiped away. Gone are the endearing ancient croft houses, or black houses, for they have been demolished or left to crumble in favour of grant-funded, modern, kit-built bungalows. These bungalows, characterless and unprepossessing from a visitor's point of view, give islanders watertight and serviced homes. On other islands, the stone croft houses, with turfed or thatched roofs, can still be seen and are protected. But on Lewis, bar a few rare exceptions, it is too late.

But while this particular heritage has vanished on Lewis, the way of life for most islanders has been inherited from the distant past. Incomes from crofting are supplemented by weaving Harris Tweed (which has to be woven by hand in islanders' homes to merit the Harris Tweed label) or by other part-time and seasonal work. Fishing remains vital, although catches have changed and are now predominantly shellfish, while some islanders have branched out into fish-farming.

Tourism is still an embryonic industry which is artificially restrained, according to island tourism agencies, by the limited capacity of ferries and aeroplanes. However, some local opinion favours the restriction of tourism anyway, believing that the intrinsic appeal of the Outer Hebrides' other-worldliness can only be preserved by such restraint. For those who do visit, white sandy beaches and a peppering of important prehistoric sites like the standing stones at Callanish on Lewis over-ride such considerations as the appalling weather (it rains on average on two days out of three in Stornoway).

Religion, whether the Catholicism practised from Benbecula southwards, or the Protestantism of the Church of Scotland and the Free Church of Scotland practised north of Benbecula, plays an unusually important role in the Western Isles. Unlike the mainland, the vast majority of islanders go to church, and many are strict Sabbatarians. As a result, especially on Lewis, buses don't operate, shops shut and hotels and bars close on Sundays out of deference to Sabbatarian opinion.

As you travel southwards from Stornoway, the political and Protestant power base, there is the distinct impression that life becomes more relaxed.

Simultaneously, facilities, such as shops, petrol stations and other services, dwindle away, and the realities of island life hit home. For all things are shipped in and many mainland necessities are by force inessential because they are unavailable. What self-sufficiency there once was (as witnessed by John Knox) has given way to importing. Crops are no longer grown extensively – crofts are grazed by sheep and cattle instead, and grants buoy up livelihoods.

Some terrain is too inhospitable to do much with. North Harris, a shock of bare lunar stone mountains, gives way to the more fertile South Harris and its wind-swept west coast sandy bays. From Harris's port, Tarbert, it is a two-hour ferry journey to North Uist's Lochmaddy, where the land flattens out. Composed of machair, sand-dunes and peat bog, North Uist is the broadest part of the thin tail of three islands which are bonded by causeways.

Driving the length of North Uist, Benbecula and South Uist, it sometimes seems as if you are travelling down one long causeway. So many lochs lap the roadside, and so much sea is crossed that it feels as though the smallest tidal rise would cover the islands altogether.

At the southern tip of South Uist, Barra is the full-stop to the Outer Hebrides. It is regarded fondly, not least because it was the model for Great Todday in Sir Compton Mackenzie's much-loved comic novel, *Whisky Galore*. The novel, based on the wrecking of the SS *Politician* just off Eriskay and the subsequent distribution of the cargo of 20,000 barrels of whisky to alcohol-starved islanders, evokes the wry humour of island existence. Barra is also well-known for its beach airstrip, which is only navigable at low tide. This is often interpreted as a haphazard symbol for haphazard island life, where the vagaries of chance and the weather are omnipotent, defeating human intentions at every turn. Samuel Johnson was perplexed by this: 'To live in perpetual want of little things, is a state not indeed of torture, but of constant vexation. I have in Skye had some difficulty to find ink for a letter; and if a woman breaks her needle, the work is at a stop.'

Mingulay

Islay (top)
Rhinns of Islay (bottom left)
Laphroaig whisky distillery, Islay (bottom right)
Lagavulin whisky distillery, Islay (opposite)

Iona
Mull (opposite, top)
Duart Castle, Mull (opposite, bottom)

The Cuillins, Skye (top)
The Storr, Skye (bottom left)
Sleat, Skye (bottom right)
Dunvegan Castle, Skye (opposite)

SY409
ALPHA
ALPHA
SY

Croft, South Uist (top)

Barra Airport, (bottom)

Stornaway harbour and boatyard, Lewis (opposite)

Roadside shrine, South Uist (above)

Standing stones, Callanish, Lewis (bottom)

Church and priest, Barra (top right)
Graveyard, Eriskay, South Uist (top left)
St Clement's Church, Rodel, Harris (bottom right)
Sir Compton Mackenzie's grave, Barra (bottom right)

Crofter, Scalpay, Harris (above)
Barra Airport (below)
Crofter, Eriskay, South Uist (opposite)

Weavers, Harris (above)

Cut peat, Lewis (below)

Tweed weaver, Tong, Lewis (opposite, top)

Cutting the peat, Lewis (opposite, bottom)

Keeper, Sumburgh Head lighthouse, Shetland

Orkney & Shetland

Separated from the Scottish mainland by the Pentland Firth, that treacherous belt of water bridging the Atlantic and the North Sea, is Orkney, an archipelago of about seventy islands, eighteen of which are inhabited. Perhaps more than any other Scottish island, Orkney somehow exists in a pocket of beguiling otherness. Its islands may seem culturally and geographically remote (they are in fact only six miles from the Scottish mainland), but their fate has been entwined with 20th-century world events.

Its reputation and appeal are multifaceted. To ornithologists and naturalists, Orkney represents a flurry of wildlife while to archaeologists, the islands are a hugely rich, largely unexcavated prehistoric site. To romantics, historical Orkney is a land with its roots in an age almost beyond our imaginations. Visually, Orkney is strikingly un-Scottish. The landscape of most islands is soothingly and uninterruptedly agricultural, a green, fertile sigh of relief after the harsh, unworkable terrain of Caithness and before the similarly intolerant landscape of Shetland.

Because the majority of the isles are flat, and therefore without the melodrama of mountains or of other photogenic Scottish trademarks, Orkney's scenery has often been underrated. George Low, a resident of Orkney who toured Orkney and Shetland in 1774, was apologetic: 'Our views in Orkney are not so romantick as elsewhere, no woods nor waters, bridges or castles, to improve the scene'.

Edwin Muir, who was born in Orkney in 1887, admits in *Scottish Journey* that the islands are not conventionally attractive but goes on to describe the special Orkney quality: '... the tourist in search of the picturesque will find little to repay him ... If he goes there in the middle of June, the long light, which never fades at that time of the year, but ebbs and ebbs until, before one can tell how, morning is there again, will charm and tease him ... If he has an eye for such things, he will be delighted by the spectacle of quickly changing skies and the clearness and brightness of all the colours ... Orkney is full of fine scenery, but that has to be looked for ...'

The Orkney islands, like their northern Shetland neighbours, offer extraordinary year-round skyscapes. So often they and the Shetland islands appear to be narrow splinters or thin wedges of land, driven in between sea and sky. As a result, the bulk of any vista is water or air, ocean or heaven. Visitors who have tasted Scandinavia will find that it is the wintertime Northern Lights and the pure, clear light of summer that ally Orkney and Shetland with Nordic countries almost more than their tangible Viking heritage.

Writing of Shetland, where he lived for some

years, Hugh MacDiarmid, poet and founder of the Scottish Nationalist Party, noted the atmospheric link: '... encompassed about with the strange beauty of the North, the fluctuation of unearthly colour at different levels of the sun, the luminous air, the gleam of distant ice, the awful stillness of Northern fog'.

Only since the late 15th century have Orkney and Shetland been under Scottish rule. Before that, the Norsemen held domain. The *Orkneyinga Saga*, believed to have been written around 1200, chronicles the violent fortunes of the Earls of Orkney. Theirs was an eventful history of conquest and exploration, and the islanders were invariably caught up in dynastic power struggles and murderous betrayals.

The tidy town of Kirkwall, Orkney's administrative centre, was founded by the Norsemen as was St Magnus Cathedral, Kirkwall's red sandstone centrepiece. The cathedral was built by Rognvald, nephew of Earl Magnus, in memory of his canonized uncle. Rather than the honourable gesture it is often understood to be, the *Orkneyinga Saga* exposes the building of the cathedral as a political manoeuvre, designed to win Orcadian support for Rognvald.

The Vikings left the islands with a legacy of placenames, but they took from Orkney too. They looted prehistoric sites like Maes Howe on Orkney's Mainland, scarring the 5000-year-old burial chamber with their 12th-century graffiti. Today, visitors are taken into the chilled belly of the grassy mound on guided tours. Perversely, the Viking act of vandalism – 'the considerable number of Norse runes scratched onto stone' – are as highly valued as the Neolithic tombs themselves.

On an grassy lip above the sandy sweep of the Bay of Skail is Skara Brae. Whipped by the wind and smashed by winter seas, the prehistoric village, some 4000 years old, is vulnerable to the elements. Visitors look down into roofless Neolithic rooms, marvelling at fireplaces, stone beds and stone sideboards while a guide explains the sophisticated drainage system and the social hierarchy: the head of the family's stone fireside chair faces the doorway and controls admissions.

Standing stones and Neolithic remains are not the sole preserve of the Mainland island: Rousay, Papa Westray, North Ronaldsay, South Ronaldsay, Stronsay, Sanday and Hoy are among the other Orkney islands that possess ancient monuments. Heather-clad Hoy, the only truly mountainous Orkney isle, has the Dwarfie Stane, a Stone Age rock tomb wedged onto the side of a hill. Its other main tourist attraction is the spectacular lone stack, the 450-foot Old Man of Hoy.

Hoy, on the western side of Scapa Flow, that notorious expanse of water ringed by islands, introduces another Orcadian theme: world war. In abandoned military buildings on Hoy, a wartime interpretation centre has been set up to tell the story of Orkney's war role. Scapa Flow was a major British naval base in both world wars and one of its best-known events was the scuttling of a large part of the surrendering German naval fleet in June 1919. The remaining wrecks are still a popular foraging ground for divers.

War left its mark on the Mainland too. Items retrieved from the German ships are on display at Stromness, perhaps the most endearing Orcadian harbour town. At Marwick Head, there is a monument to British War Secretary Lord Kitchener, who died in 1916 when his ship went down off the Orkney coast under mysterious circumstances; following much speculation and investigation, it is now commonly believed that a German mine was to blame.

A positive war benefit to islanders came after repeated attempts in both world wars to block the eastern entrance to the Scapa Flow with defunct ships (rusty hulks still jut out of the water). The strategic importance of controlling Scapa Flow finally resulted in the construction of the Churchill

Barriers, causeways which join the inhabited islands of Burray and South Ronaldsay to the Mainland.

It is hard to believe that peaceful villages like Burray Village or the pretty harbour of St Margaret's Hope on South Ronaldsay were ever in the front-line of war. Contemporary life is generally calm: the industries of farming, fishing, tourism and crafts are pursued with steady commitment.

A relatively recent financial input has come from North Sea oil. There is a large on-shore oil terminal, with a rash of pot-bellied storage tanks, on Flotta. Yet the traces of North Sea oil money are less visible on Orkney than they are on Shetland, where leisure centres in particular have sprouted in unlikely, sparsely-populated places. It is perhaps true to say that Shetland, with its economic dependence on the unpredictable crofting and fishing industries, and with its barren, boggy terrain, has more need of oil revenue than Orkney. Shetland's oil magnet, the biggest oil and liquified gas terminal in Europe, is at Sullom Voe in the north of the Mainland.

One thousand miles from London and two hundred miles from Norway, Shetland is more vociferous about its Norse connections than Orkney. It has its own flag, a white Scandinavian cross on a background of Scottish blue. There are Shetlanders who would like the islands to come under Norwegian rule once more and there are activists who labour to keep the Norn dialect alive. The monthly magazine, *Shetland Life*, carries poems in Norn, as well as a column on Norwegian life. 'Don't Drop Litter' signs are written in wonderfully onomatopoeic Norn: 'Dunna Chuck Bruck'.

The best known look backwards to a Viking past is the Up Helly Aa festival which celebrates the return of the sun, held on the last Tuesday of every January. It involves a torchlight procession through Lerwick, 900 men in fancy dress, a squad of Vikings and the burning of a Viking longship. For islanders, the highest honour is to be amongst the party of Vikings. They are elected, and it takes 25 years from the time of election to the time of performance.

As well as its colourful Norse heritage, Shetland is famed for its more prosaic knitwear and ponies. The latter, still to be seen all over the islands, were objects of fascination even in the 18th century. George Low recorded in his 1774 journal that the stubby, reputedly bad-tempered ponies were 'much bought by strangers as curiosities, and for children'. Today, breeders' sales still pull large, inquisitive crowds.

Knitwear remains an important supplement to islanders' incomes. There are mechanised factories producing cable sweaters on Shetland's Mainland; knitwear sold under the 'Shetland Lady' trademark will be bona fide Shetland products. The familiar patterns – 'the neck-to-shoulder necklace of colour' – are invariably handmade and knitted at home, as are the intricate designs of Fair Isle cardigans. Because of the amount of work involved, it is not unknown for demand for handmade Shetland knitwear to outstrip supply.

Although revenue from the oil fields is subsidising many community projects, fishing is still sustained as the staple industry. The harbour at Scalloway and the large one at Lerwick, sheltered by the island of Bressay, are the main trawler landing stations.

All pedestrian routes in Lerwick, the landing place for ferries from the Scottish mainland, lead down to the harbourside. The old part of the town is a warren of stone-stepped alleyways, scarcely wide enough for one person. Several climb down from Fort Charlotte, a walled 18th-century defensive post set above the harbour with a grassy apron which serves as a fine viewing point.

Of Shetland's ancient monuments, the 43-foot high broch or defensive tower on the island of Mousa, and Jarlshof, on the Mainland, usually top the tourist itinerary. Jarlshof, a grassy site beside the bay of West Voe and near Sumburgh Airport, exposes the historical layers of settlement. The foundations of a 4000-year-old hut and of Bronze Age, Iron Age and Norse dwellings have been uncovered and can be viewed from wooden platforms. The largest surviving building was described by Sir Walter Scott in his journal as 'the old house at Sumburgh ... a most dreary mansion'. It appears in his novel *The Pirate*, where the name 'Jarlshof' was first used – a fictitious title which has stuck fast.

Like Orkney, Shetland was of crucial strategic importance during the First and Second World Wars when ships and servicemen were based in the islands. During German occupation of Norway in the Second World War, the Norwegian Resistance movement operated out of Shetland – a cooperation which strengthened the emotional ties between Shetland and Norway.

Of the 100 Shetland isles, only a small number are inhabited. The North Isles – Yell, Unst and Fetlar – are the largest, but even they struggle to keep their population levels up. In early 1991, Fetlar advertised in national magazines for new residents who might be prepared to take up the challenge of island life.

Like Orkney, Shetland's Mainland, its smaller islands and Fetlar, Unst and Yell prove irresistible to ornithologists. Monitored carefully by the Shetland Bird Club and the Royal Society for the Protection of Birds, troops of binocular-wielding enthusiasts trek across cliffs and headlands in search of the colonies of seabirds, which range from puffins to the Great Skua (known locally as the bonxie). There are two National Nature Reserves, one at Hermaness on Unst and one on the island of Noss.

Shetland is the true home of the naturalist in search of unspoilt wilderness, of those who appreciate in landscapes what Hugh MacDiarmid called 'a certain asceticism' and of those who can perceive 'the infinite beauties of bare land and the shapes and colours of the rocks.'

St Magnus Cathedral, Kirkwall, Orkney (above and opposite)

NO URANIUM
KEEP ORKNEY GREEN & ATTRACTIVE
NOT WHITE & RADIO-ACTIVE

Ring of Brodgar, Orkney (above)
Skara Brae, Orkney (right)
Stromness, Orkney (opposite, top)
Furzbreck pottery, Orkney (opposite, bottom left)
Roadsign, Stromness (opposite, bottom right)
Mac Bain, tangle-gatherer, Stromness (opposite, bottom right)

Block Ship, Hoy (top)

Italian Chapel, Lamb Holm, Orkney (bottom)

The Old Man of Hoy, Orkney (opposite)

Hoy (top)
Scallops and partans (bottom left and right)

Rousay and Eynhallow Sound, Orkney (top)
Croft, South Ronaldsay, Orkney (bottom)

ALBERT BUILDING
LK 472

Croft, Shetland (top)
Jarlshof, Shetland (bottom)
Flotta, Orkney (opposite, top)
Lerwick harbour, Shetland (opposite, bottom)

Crofter, Shetland (top)

Stained glass, St Margaret's Church, Lerwick (bottom left and right)

Fiddler, Shetland (bottom centre)

Shetland ponies (above)
Stained glass, Lerwick Town Hall (right)
Lerwick fishing boat (far right)
Home knitters, Shetland (below & overleaf)

My sincere thanks go to the many individuals and organisations for the kindness and generosity shown to me during my travels taking the photographs for this book.

KEITH ALLARDYCE